the ELEPHANT *in the* PEW

A Woman's Guide to Freedom from Lust, Frigidity, and Sexual Dysfunction

Published in Windsor, Ontario, Canada by Barbara De Simon and makeyourselfready.com—a Kingdom-focused Christian ministry equipping women to submit to the King of kings and fulfill their call in their sphere of influence.

This book is not intended to be a substitute for the advice of medical professionals. Please seek the help of a certified therapist for extreme cases of abuse such as RSA (ritual satanic abuse). It is the responsibility of the reader to seek professional help when needed, at their own discretion. This book is written for Christians who have committed their lives to be a disciple of Christ, not for anyone else. Those who are not committed to Christ cannot and are not expected to apply any of these teachings or prayers.

Interior design and full cover by Barbara De Simon. Front cover image from CHATGPT.

ISBN: 978-1-7383840-9-9

DEDICATION

This book is written in honor of my beautiful late mother, Ella May, who suffered sexual abuse but did not experience emotional healing from it until she crossed over into the arms of Jesus on May 13, 2010. In honor of my Jesus and my mom, I will stand against abuse and its emotional trauma to break the demonic power at its source so others can come into the freedom Jesus died for. I will be the breaker generation in my family whom The Master Breaker can work through and say, "No more! It's come this far but now I draw a holy bloodline in the sand with my Jesus. It stops with me."

TABLE OF CONTENTS

INTRODUCTION

Do you remember what the two apostles who walked along the road to Emmaus said in Luke 24:32, when they suddenly realized that the stranger who had walked with them was the resurrected Christ? "Did not our heart burn within us while He talked with us on the road, and while He opened the Scriptures to us?" This is how I feel about the message I'm about to write in this book; it is such a needed word in this hour, and it's burning to be released so it can bring freedom to many.

Our world, all around us, media, every sphere of influence, is saturated with lust and perversion. Everywhere I turn, there's sexual innuendo at the very least but in movies and TV, there's blatant sexual perversion and full nakedness on display leaving nothing to the imagination. It is affecting us all, making our consciousness numb to it so we accept more of it without restriction. Some shows on Netflix now, in my opinion, should be categorized as pornography; it's that graphic.

There's a thought or an assumption out there that I don't think is true. The assumption is that women don't struggle with lust—that it's strictly a man's problem. Speaking as a woman who once struggled with intrusive perverse thoughts and dreams, I'm not buying it. I'm not swallowing that pill. I think it's just not something that is talked about. It's something that women are not free to admit because there's so much stigma and shame attached to it—even more than the shame attached to men's lust issues. Why? Because women have been expected to be a certain way. Right? We are expected to not like sex. The stereotypical female fakes a headache when her husband wants to be intimate. But the ever so "awakened" sexual culture nowadays and of the last ten to fifteen years has formed the hearts and minds of young women all over, bent toward perversity more than purity. Now, it's a woman problem just as much a man problem. Now the struggle is real for us too. Now we pay the price of sexual liberality introduced into the school system. Perversion isn't just affecting men. It's affecting women and I am giving you, woman of God, permission to admit it, talk about it with the Lord and allow Him to unravel it, dismantle it and kick it out, so you can be free.

As we explore this topic, I will be vulnerable with you, so you know you're not alone. We will learn what is at the root of the struggle and also where these issues can start, so you can, with the help of the Holy Spirit, identify where your own struggle began. Somewhere, perversity took root in your mind—intimacy, love, and sex got twisted in your thinking and perspective. But there is no need to wring your hands over it any longer. There is no need to wallow in a pit of shame anymore. Freedom is only days away. Freedom is as close as your willingness to admit it, confront it, and pray it through with the Holy Spirit.

Do you know that scripture in Romans 7 when Paul cries out, "What a wretched man I am! Who will rescue me from this body that is subject to death?" (Romans 7:24 NIV). Well just before that in verse 15 he says, "I do not understand what I do. For what I want to do I do not do, but what I hate I do" (Romans 7:15 NIV). Have you ever felt that frustration? I know it well. You go to bed in a good frame of mind and wake up from a dream no one should ever have, let alone a Christian woman, with so much guilt and shame. You cry out in frustration, "Why! Why does this keep happening to me?" It's like after you fall asleep something else takes over. For some, Romans 7:15 feels like a life-verse; the struggle is so intense. It feels like you will never be free. But I declare to you now, it's NOT your life-verse! You WILL NOT struggle your whole life in this same fight. The Lord has deliverance for you. Paul says right after, "Who will rescue me from this body that is subject to death?" (Romans 7:24b NIV) "Thanks be to God, who delivers me through Jesus Christ our Lord!" (Romans 7:25a NIV). Hallelujah! God delivers us, and He's about to deliver you.

Throughout the pages of this book, we will learn how to come into agreement with and experience deliverance, for real, through the power of the Spirit. It won't be just talk. It won't be just an empty promise. It will be a new reality of freedom that you walk in and live, with joy. You will celebrate and exclaim, "My God has set me free! I am no longer tormented by thoughts and dreams I don't want to have. I am really and truly free! And I know my God now, like I've never known Him before. He has revealed Himself to me as my Deliverer, Healer, Good Father, and friend."

I also love Romans 8:1-2. These *are my* life-verses for sure. And before I type them out here for you, take note that these verses come directly after Romans 7—the verses we just looked at above.

Romans 8:1-2 says:

> Therefore, there is now *no condemnation* for those who are *in Christ Jesus*, because through Christ Jesus the law of the Spirit who gives life has set you free from the law of sin and death. (NIV, emphasis added)

This means, for us, who have surrendered our lives to Jesus Christ, who are now re-born, made brand-new[1] and hidden inside of the identity of Christ Jesus, there is no longer any condemnation against us. No matter what we do, think, or dream, we are forgiven, as we continue to live a lifestyle of submission, confession, and repentance. And we've been given the empowerment needed through the Spirit, Who gives life, to say "no" to sin. We have been set free from the law of sin and death; we are no longer *bound* to it but bound to a new LAW—the law of the Spirit of Life. Now, at times, it may *feel* like we can't say "no" to sin, but this is simply an indication that we need deliverance from a sin *habit* which our *flesh* may have enjoyed in the past and possibly an opposing spirit like *lust* or *perversion* which can keep us stuck giving into temptation. (But don't worry, we'll get into that discussion later. It's not as complicated or intimidating as you think. Jesus is always greater!)

Who should read this book? Well, I have written this book for women, but men get free from the same thing, the same way, so they would benefit from it as well. However, *my* focus right now is my sisters-in-Christ. The following is a list of who would benefit from reading this book:

- Those having intrusive, sexually perverse thoughts or dreams.
- Those convicted by the Holy Spirit to stop any type of sexual act or lifestyle, they are currently involved in but can't seem to break free from, through willpower alone.
- Those struggling with any type of sexual addiction, whether it be self-gratification (masturbation) or pornography.
- Those tempted to watch pornography.
- Those having vivid sexual dreams to the point where they feel physically violated.
- Those aware of sexual abuse or dysfunction, lust and perversion in their family-line back through the generations.

- Those completely turned off by sex or those who hate sex.
- Those who have suffered sexual molestation or abuse.
- Those who have been raped or experienced non-consensual sex with anyone, including a boyfriend.

In order to benefit from reading this book though, one should put it into practice by praying, in faith, through the prayers presented, with all their heart and authority they have in Jesus. The result of your heart agreement and participation is freedom from temptation and the influence of demonic entities connected to lust and perversion. A person may say, "Well, I experienced sexual abuse when I was young, but I'm not tempted to sin sexually," should still work through this book to ensure they are not tempted unexpectedly in the future *or* carrying wrong attitudes about sex and possibly not enjoying sex or being "frigid" toward their husband. ("Frigid" meaning cold, unresponsive or uninterested in sex.)

That was a heavy list, wasn't it. It could have been fairly triggering for some. Did you find your heart beating a little faster or your emotions getting stirred up as you read some of those points or situations? If so, sorry to bring it up friend. There are some things we just want to keep buried. Right? To forget about? Pretend never happened? I know. It's so very difficult to face these issues. I get it. I have walked through multiple stages of healing from *non-consensual sex (date-rape)* including: hate toward the perpetrator, forgiving the perpetrator, overcoming shame, recovering my dignity and the time spent living as a victim, forgiving myself for the sin that enabled the situation (drunkenness in particular), receiving God's forgiveness in its fullness, and finally being delivered from spirits of lust, rape, and perversion—all sovereignly orchestrated by God Himself. I did not have a book to read about recovery. I did not have a plan, and *for the most part*, I did not have a mentor or pastor leading me through the process. It was all God and His divine intervention and power as I sought Him in my own prayer and devotional life. It was all Him. He loved me so much, He just stepped right in, led me through it, and made the healing happen.

God is in the healing business—not just the healing of our spirit through re-birth, but the healing of our mind, will, and emotions—the healing of our entire inner man. He wants us whole. He wants us well in every way. And in particular, He wants *you* well in every way. He wants *you* to have a healthy and righteous view of sex *and* desire for sex as He created and intended. And He wants *you* to be empowered through His Spirit to live a righteous and holy life.

In closing, I find Psalms 32 quite fitting for this book. King David wrote this Psalm, and he may very well have written it after confessing his sin with Bathsheba (see 2nd Samuel 11).

In short, King David did not go out to battle when he was supposed to and while at home he saw a woman on her rooftop bathing. He sent for her and had sexual relations with her, causing her to become pregnant. He then called her husband, Uriah, to come home from battle to rest, hoping he would be intimate with his wife while there. Unfortunately, Uriah refused to enjoy *anything* while his comrades were fighting. So, to not be caught in his sin, David came up with another plan. He sent instruction to the battle commander to put Uriah on the frontlines where the fiercest warriors fought, on purpose, so Uriah might be killed. Unfortunately for Uriah, King David's plan was successful. After Bathsheba mourned for her husband, King David took her to be his wife, but King David was not off the hook as he hoped because what he had done displeased the Lord (2nd Samuel 11:27). When we are in relationship with God, He will keep us accountable! And that He did with King David (see 2nd Samuel 12) by sending His Prophet, Nathan, to confront him. King David did finally repent and confess his sin to God. Here's part of Psalms 32 for you to contemplate:

> Blessed is he whose transgression is forgiven, whose sin is covered. Blessed is the man to whom the Lord does not impute iniquity, and in whose spirit there is no deceit. When I kept silent, my bones grew old through my groaning all the day long. For day and night Your hand was heavy upon me; My vitality was turned into the drought of summer. I acknowledged my sin to You, and my iniquity I have not hidden. I said, "I will confess my transgressions to the LORD," and You forgave the iniquity of my sin. For this cause everyone who is godly shall pray to You in a time when You may be found; Surely in a flood of great waters they shall not come near him. You are my hiding place; You shall preserve me from trouble; You shall surround me with songs of deliverance. (Psalms 32:1-7)

Such a great Word for us now. Never hold on to the guilt of your sin and/or iniquity (more on the difference later). Go to God. Confess to Him what is heavy on your heart and repent—turn around, change your mind, and head back into the arms of your loving heavenly Father. He is always ready to receive you with love, mercy, and grace. He is so long-suffering.

What does long-suffering mean? It means *having or showing patience in spite of troubles, especially those caused by other people* (bing.com). In other words, the Lord shows patience to and for you repeatedly, giving you all the chances you need to fully recover and live for Him, being holy just as He is holy.

Thanks for picking up this book friend, despite how awkward it may have felt. Join me, whole-heartedly, as we take this journey to freedom together, under His eternal, never-ending, powerful, and restoring waterfall of grace.

---

[1] 2nd Corinthians 5:17, "Therefore, if anyone is in Christ, he is a new creation; old things have passed away; behold, all things have become new."

1

THE REALITY OF THE SPIRIT REALM

The thief does not come except to steal, and to kill, and to destroy. I have come that they may have life, and that they may have it more abundantly. (John 10:10)

I've heard it said, "What you don't know won't hurt you." This is completely false. And I'm sure you realize that. We all can be in harms way from things that we are unaware of. A toddler doesn't know that a hot stove will burn him/her, but when they touch the stove, they are burned all the same; this is why parents teach their children to be wise and "don't touch the stove!"

I've also heard some say, "I'll believe it when I see it." This is the world's way. Isn't it? It's the opposite of faith. Hebrews 11:1 says, "Now faith is the substance of things hoped for, the evidence of things *not* seen" (emphasis added). Faith is what produces the substance and the evidence of that which we believe for and hope for. Hallelujah! Faith is what pulls God's promises which are not yet seen, into our reality. Jesus said in John 20:29, *"...Blessed are those who have not seen and yet have believed."*

God's promises are true. They are true when we see the fruit of them, but they are also true *before* we see the fruit. Right?

Seeing the fruit doesn't make them true; God's Word and His faithfulness make them true. He is true to His Word.

Many times, however, Christians want to pick and choose which truth they believe. If it makes them uncomfortable, they just skim over those passages and concentrate on the ones they like. Some people are happy to believe in the truth of the existence of God, and the victory of Jesus, but don't *want* to believe in the truth of the existence of the enemy and his ability to influence them—even though scripture clearly tells them this is so. And I get it. It's a bit unnerving, especially when one doesn't understand who they have become in Christ and the authority Christ has given them over the demonic realm (when they are *truly* born-again).

I remember when I was first born-again and surrendered my life to Christ at the age of twenty-two. I came out of a religion that didn't believe in the devil and when I began to do a Bible study on Ephesians 6 with my small group, I got a little freaked out. When I was baptized in the Holy Spirit, all my spiritual senses opened, and I began to sense things in the atmosphere. I would sit at home doing my Bible study and suddenly feel like someone was watching me. I'd look up and look around with my skin crawling and the hair on the back of my neck standing straight up. I had to learn who I was fast, in order to shut down the fear that tried to grip me. Reading the books by Neil T. Anderson called, *Victory Over the Darkness* and *Bondage Breaker* was crucial for my understanding and ability to move forward in truth. (More on who we are in Christ in the next chapter.)

We only need to read Ephesians 6:10-18, as follows, to hear the truth that we do indeed have an enemy and the truth of who he really is:

> Finally, my brethren, be strong in the Lord and in the power of His might. Put on the whole armor of

> God, that you may be able to stand against the wiles of the devil. For we do not wrestle against flesh and blood, but against *principalities*, against *powers*, against *the rulers of the darkness of this age*, against *spiritual hosts of wickedness* in the heavenly places. Therefore take up the whole armor of God, that you may be able to withstand in the evil day, and having done all, to stand. Stand therefore, having girded your waist with truth, having put on the breastplate of righteousness, and having shod your feet with the preparation of the gospel of peace; above all, taking the shield of faith with which you will be able to quench all the fiery darts of the wicked one. And take the helmet of salvation, and the sword of the Spirit, which is the word of God; praying always with all prayer and supplication in the Spirit, being watchful to this end with all perseverance and supplication for all the saints—" (emphasis added).

We don't wrestle against flesh and blood. Other people are not our enemies, though at times it may seem like it. No. Instead, we wrestle against:

- Principalities;
- Powers;
- Rulers of the darkness of this age;
- Spiritual hosts of wickedness;

all of which are in the heavenly realm or the spirit realm, invisible to the natural eye. Just in case you were wondering, "What actually is a Principality?" A "Principality" is a chief "prince" demon that rules in a geographical territory. Here's an interesting scripture in Ephesians 2:1-2:

> "And you *He made alive*, who were dead in trespasses and sins, in which you once walked

> according to the course of this world, according to the *prince of the power of the air*, the spirit who now works in the sons of disobedience…" (emphasis added).

Notice the phrase, *"the prince of the power of the air."* First, this tells us that there is *power* in the air. Next, it tells us that there is a *"prince"* who rules the power of the air. This *"prince"* is not the Holy Spirit because we read that this is the "spirit who now works in the sons of *disobedience*." There is a multitude of spiritual entities all around us in the atmosphere.

Also, we can look at 1 Peter 5:8-9 as follows:

> Be sober, be vigilant; because your adversary the devil walks about like a roaring lion, seeking whom he may devour. Resist him, steadfast in the faith, knowing that the same sufferings are experienced by your brotherhood in the world.

This scripture, in 1 Peter 1:1-2a, is addressed to "the pilgrims of the Dispersion in Pontus, Galatia, Cappadocia, Asia, and Bithynia, elect according to the foreknowledge of God the Father, in sanctification of the Spirit…" *"Pilgrims of the Dispersion"* was a common designation used to apply to Christian Jews scattered by persecution and Peter, in particular, also used it to refer to converted Gentiles who had been scattered in the same way.[2] So, my point is, 1 Peter was written to Christians—those who were already converted—in fact, "the *elect* according to the foreknowledge of God the Father" undergoing sanctification.

A *roaring lion* is an aggressive predator, isn't it? It's not passive. A *roaring lion* is intimidating and ferocious, showing no mercy. In fact, the purpose of a lion roaring is to exert dominance, instill fear, and defend its territory. Friends, the enemy continually tries to intimidate us, and he is looking for any opportunity to attack and oppress us. Our job is to be sober, be vigilant and not give him *any* opportunity to oppress us. We can't get away from his temptation totally, but we can and are to resist (James 4:7) and overcome so he can't oppress us or enslave us again, just as he did before we were saved (Galatians 5:1).

We must understand that the demonic realm is real and we, as believers, are its target. Demons hate us. Yes, Jesus has destroyed the works of the devil[3], and He has set us free from the *rule* of the devil, but the devil is still the *god of this world.*[4] And the devil is a liar, a thief, and a lawbreaker; he regularly attempts to encroach upon territory that no longer belongs to him; he can act like a *squatter*.

A *squatter* is someone who trespasses, breaks into a home and unlawfully occupies a home or property that he/she does not legally have any right to occupy. In the natural, this happens because the homeowner has left it vacant and has not stewarded the upkeep and maintenance of the home. It has become abandoned; no one has been watching, paying attention, or maintaining it. This can be easily compared to the neglect of our physical, emotional, mental, spiritual, and sexual health. Have we been on guard? Have we been aware of ourselves and our activity—watching what we take in and put out—think and speak? The devil is sneaky; he can very easily infiltrate an area we haven't been stewarding.

It is also true that because we have free-will, we oversee ourselves and have the responsibility to partner with the Holy Spirit and His power, to live holy lives. But it is very possible for us to slip up—to make a mistake, as we are not yet perfected. If we get busy with life, work, school, kids, chores, family, and church, perhaps we haven't taken the time to pray and repent and allow the Holy Spirit to search our heart. This is dangerous; we must keep short accounts with God. Anything or area that we have been convicted of but have not repented for provides the enemy with LEGAL ground to encroach on and gives him rights to cause us grief and strife. We must watch and obey. We must live a life of abiding in Christ, in constant prayer and surrender to His Lordship, taking the time to recharge in Him and unload the junk we may have accumulated over the course of our day, in repentance. The devil is a thief, but he is also a legalist when it serves him. He will use what he can against us to give him legal right.

The devil will also use the Word of God in a way that it was not intended, much like he did with Jesus in the wilderness when he tempted Jesus to throw Himself off a cliff. Satan said to Jesus in Matthew 4:6, "...*If* You are the Son of God, throw Yourself down. For it is written: 'He shall give His angels charge over you,' and 'In their hands they shall bear you up, lest You dash your foot against a stone." Satan quotes Psalms 91:11-12 but uses it to justify sinful actions. Jesus knew better than to *purposely* throw Himself off a cliff as this would be testing or "tempting" God. In fact, what Jesus said in response to Satan in Matthew 4:7, "...You shall not tempt the Lord your God," is also a quote from the Word, found in Deuteronomy 6:16. The only reason to put God to the test is to prove His faithfulness which is in itself proof of doubt and unbelief on behalf of the one doing the testing. It would be sin. But I digress. My point is that the devil knows the Word of God. And He knows how to twist it and take it out of context in order to put us in bondage to a lie. We must know by the Spirit how to divide or discern correctly and apply the Word of truth. The scripture II Timothy 2:15 says, "Be diligent to present yourself approved to God, a worker who does not need to be ashamed, rightly dividing the word of truth."

So how does the demonic realm affect us? We can't see it… usually. But we can feel it at times. Have you ever toured a house while house hunting and discerned that something was off—something felt a little creepy? You couldn't quite put your finger on it. Nothing obvious or in the physical realm was wrong, but something sure was wrong in the spiritual realm. You felt it. And you couldn't wait to get out of there.

We can also *hear* the spirit realm at times—not with our natural ears but inside our mind. Have you ever had a thought just pop into your mind that made you go, *that was random!* Or, *oh my Lord, why would I think that? What is wrong with me?* Yes? Me too. Well, I have learned that not all thoughts that come into my mind are me. Some are. And some are from God. But some are directly from the demons in the atmosphere.

Let's look at the interaction between Jesus and Peter in Matthew 16. Beginning in verse 13, Jesus asks His disciples, "Who do men say that I, the Son of Man, am?" The disciples respond, but then Jesus asks His disciples who *they* think He is. Simon Peter responds and says, "You are the Christ, the Son of the living God" (Matt. 16:16). This is a win for Peter! Jesus says to him, "Blessed are you, Simon Bar-Jonah, for flesh and blood has not revealed this to you, but My Father who is in heaven" (Matt. 16:17). Peter knew the truth of who Jesus truly was, but he did not learn that from *"flesh and blood."* Peter didn't get that knowledge from a podcast he listened to nor did he get it from Bible college. He got that revelation straight from the Father, via the Holy Spirit, speaking to his heart and mind. (It's your heart (spirit) that bears witness that you are indeed hearing God's voice.)

Now, jump down to verses 21-23, in Matthew 16. Same chapter! We see something else influencing Peter's thoughts. Jesus begins to share with the disciples that He was going to suffer and die but then be raised up again on the third day. But Peter didn't like that idea, and he came into agreement with another thought.

> Then Peter took Him aside and began to rebuke Him, saying, "Far be it from You, Lord; this shall not happen to You! But He turned and said to Peter, "Get behind Me, Satan! You are an offense to Me, for you are not *mindful* of the things of God, but the things of men." (Matthew 16:22-23, emphasis added)

Ouch! Wow. Jesus is speaking a different tune over Peter now. "Get behind Me, Satan!" The ultimate rebuke. But don't get offended on Peter's behalf. Jesus was not calling Peter, Satan. On the contrary, Jesus loved Peter, but He knew that the *influence* behind Peter's declaration was Satan—that the source was a thought planted in Peter's mind by the demonic realm. Look at Jesus' statement, "…for you are not *mindful of the things of God…*" Peter's mind was no longer full of revelation from God, but full of *"the things of men"* coming from the demonic realm. His mind was full of what he wanted, not what God wanted. The number one temptation Satan uses is the selfish desires of men—the things that please a man's soul or flesh.

Let's look at 2nd Corinthians 10:4-5. "For the weapons of our warfare are not carnal but mighty in God for…" what? What are the weapons for? The next part tells us, "…pulling down strongholds, casting down arguments and every high thing that exalts itself against the knowledge of God." How do we pull these things down? We bring every thought captive to the obedience of Christ (2nd Cor. 10:5). The strongholds are in our mind. The arguments, reasonings, and lies that exalt themselves against the truth of God are in our mind. And they are planted there by the demons lurking all around us.

A *stronghold* is a fortified place in the mind—a well-worn path (neuropathway) which has formed around a lie or a series of lies that we have believed. A spirit of deception keeps it established until through prayer and the power of the Holy Spirit, we repent and begin to take our thoughts captive—to actively examine our thoughts for truth and lies, asking whether our thoughts are godly and whether they are in alignment with the truth of the Word. The battle is in the mind where we must *field* our thoughts, discerning whether to rebuke them, throw them in the trash or to embrace and act on them.

This is not meant to cause paranoia or fear. We have the authority over the devil in Christ, but we must be aware of his schemes. We must not be ignorant nor try to ignore what the devil does or is capable of. Trying to ignore it will only make it worse. We are told to resist him and "stand" against him.

Okay, hopefully you dear reader, are on board with the truth that the demonic spirit realm is real and that we are all, indeed, in an unseen battle to submit to God, resist the devil, and make him flee![5]

The next step for us before we get any deeper is to make sure we understand what Jesus has accomplished for us on the cross and who we have become as daughters of God, which equips us, quite radically, to stand against the enemy.

The next chapter, *Who's Who*, is adapted from my previous book, *Spiritual Protection and Deliverance for our Children.*

---

[2] The Woman's Study Bible, New King James Version, Thomas Nelson, 2006, page 1628.

[3] "And you, being dead in your trespasses and the uncircumcision of your flesh, He has made alive together with Him, having forgiven you all trespasses, having wiped out the handwriting of requirements that was against us, which was contrary to us. And He has taken it out of the way, having nailed it to the cross. Having disarmed principalities and powers, He made a public spectacle of them, triumphing over them in it" (Colossians 2:13-15). "The Son of God appeared for this purpose, to destroy the works of the devil" (I John 3:8b AMP).

[4] "If the Good News we preach is hidden behind a veil, it is hidden only from people who are perishing. Satan, who is the god of this world, has blinded the minds of those who don't believe" (2 Cor. 4:3-4a NLT).

[5] "Where do wars and fights come from among you? Do they not come from your desires for pleasure that war in your members? You lust and do not have. You murder and covet and cannot obtain. You fight and war. Yet you do not have because you do not ask. You ask and do not receive, because you ask amiss, that you may spend it on your pleasures. Adulterers and adulteresses! Do you not know that friendship with the world is enmity with God? Whoever therefore wants to be a friend of the world makes himself an enemy of God. Or do you think that the Scripture says in vain, "The Spirit who dwells in us yearns jealously? But He gives more grace. Therefore He says: "God resists the proud, but gives grace to the humble." Therefore submit to God. Resist the devil and he will flee from you" (James 4:1-7).

2

WHO'S WHO

He was in the world, and the world was made through Him, and the world did not know Him. He came to His own, and His own did not receive Him. But as many as received Him, to them He gave the right to become children of God, to those who believe in His name... (John 1:10-12)

This chapter right here is going to give you the most important truths you can use to enforce and defend the victory Christ has already won on your behalf. Get your highlighter out and ready to go! Let's consider who is who in this cosmic battle between good and evil.

WHO IS GOD?

God Almighty, Elohim, Jehovah, The Beginning and The End, The Great I Am, The Creator of all, He is supreme, rules over all and He is the most important, most powerful participant. He has always existed and is completely independent all on His own; He doesn't need anything or anyone although He loves us and created us to bring Him glory. Acts 17:24-25 says:

> God, who made the world and everything in it, since He is Lord of heaven and earth, does not dwell in temples made with hands. Nor is He worshipped with men's hands, as though He

> needed anything, since He gives to all life, breath, and all things.

God is faithful and does not change in character or in His purposes; His character and His purposes remain the same. This means we can trust Him forever. James 1:17 says, "Every good gift and every perfect gift is from above, and comes down from the Father of lights, with whom there is no variation or shadow of turning." Hebrews 13:8 says, "Jesus Christ is the same yesterday, today, and forever." And we know that Jesus is the exact representation of the Father as Jesus said to Philip in John 14:9, "...Anyone who has seen me has seen the Father..."

God is omnipresent—everywhere all the time, without size or spatial dimensions. God is omnipotent—all powerful and omniscient; He knows everything. God is preeminent, surpassing all others.

And my favorite: God is love and God is good, all the time. He is exceedingly merciful. First John 4:16 says, "And we have known and believed the love that God has for us. God is love, and he who abides in love abides in God, and God in him."

God is also just. He is a good and faithful judge. Here's Job 37:5-13 describing His great power over the earth:

> God thunders marvelously with His voice; He does great things which we cannot comprehend. For He says to the snow, 'Fall on the earth;' Likewise to the gentle rain and the heavy rain of His strength. He seals the hand of every man, that all men may know His work. The beasts go into dens, and remain in their lairs. From the chamber *of the south* comes the whirlwind, And cold from the scattering winds *of the north*. By the breath of God ice is given, And the broad waters are frozen. Also with

> moisture He saturates the thick clouds; He scatters His bright clouds. And they swirl about, being turned by His guidance, that they may do whatever He commands them on the face of the whole earth. He causes it to come, whether for correction, or for His land, or for mercy.

God, Jesus and the Holy Spirit are all equal in their majesty and power. They differ in their function, but they are all in harmony and agreement with one another. Jesus and Holy Spirit submit completely to the Father and do His bidding perfectly.

WHO IS SATAN?

Satan is a created being (created by God), a fallen angel who began as an archangel named Lucifer.

It's a very common mindset to think about God and Satan as being opposite one another—good and evil. But this mindset leads us to also think that God and Satan are equal in power, when they are emphatically not.

God is the Creator and Satan is the creation. No creation is ever greater or even equal to its creator—ever. In fact, the creation is always subject to its creator. Let's consider this by looking at Job 1:6-7:

> Now there was a day when the sons of God (angels) came to present themselves before the LORD, and Satan (adversary, accuser) also came among them. The LORD said to Satan, "From where have you come?" Then Satan answered the LORD, "From roaming around on the earth and from walking around on it" (AMP).

As we continue to read in Job, God asks Satan if he had considered Job—if he had noticed how upright Job is. God brags on Job as if to tempt Satan into sifting him. Satan says to God:

> Does Job fear God for nothing? Have you not put a hedge around him and his household and everything he has? You have blessed the work of his hands, so that his flock and herds are spread throughout the land. But now stretch out your hand and strike everything he has, and he will surely curse you to your face. (Job 1:9 NIV)

In verse twelve God responds, "Very well, then, everything he has is in your power, but on the man himself do not lay a finger" (Job 1:12 NIV). We see from this exchange that God holds the power, and Satan cannot do anything to Job without God's consent. In essence we see that God has Satan on a very short leash. The important takeaway from all this is even *before* Jesus overcame all demonic powers on our behalf at the cross, Satan could not just do whatever he wanted; he was subject to God.

It is suggested by some theologians that Lucifer was the leader of worship on the mountain of the Lord. Here's Ezekiel 28:12b-16 which describes who Satan was in heaven and his unfortunate rebellion:

> "You *were* the seal of perfection, full of wisdom and perfect in beauty. You were in Eden, the garden of God; every precious stone *was* your covering: the sardius, topaz, and diamond, beryl, onyx, and jasper, sapphire, turquoise, and emerald with gold. The workmanship of your timbrels and pipes was prepared for you on the day you were created. You *were* the anointed cherub who covers; I established you; you were on the holy mountain of God; you walked back and forth in the midst of fiery stones. You were perfect in your ways from the day you

> were created, till iniquity was found in you. "By the abundance of your trading you became filled with violence within, and you sinned; Therefore I cast you as a profane thing out of the mountain of God; and I destroyed you, O covering cherub, from the midst of the fiery stones.

Also, portions of Isaiah 14, which describes the king of Babylon, goes beyond describing an earthly king to describing the spiritual power behind that king—Satan himself:

> "How you are fallen from heaven, O Lucifer, son of the morning! *How* you are cut down to the ground, you who weakened the nations! For you have said in your heart: 'I will ascend into heaven, I will exalt my throne above the stars of God; I will also sit on the mount of the congregation on the farthest sides of the north; I will ascend above the heights of the clouds, I will be like the Most High.' (Isaiah 14:12-14)

So, we know that Satan was kicked out of heaven and took a third of the angels with him (Revelation 12:4-9). In the New Testament, he is called *"the god of this world"* (2 Cor. 4:4), *"the thief"* (John 10:10), and the *"father of lies."* Jesus tells us about his nature in John 8:44:

> You belong to your father, the devil, and you want to carry out your father's desires. He was a murderer from the beginning, not holding to the truth, for there is no truth in him. When he lies, he speaks his native language, for he is a liar and the father of lies (NIV).

The good news in all of this is that Jesus took him on and overcame, disarming the enemy and all his minions, making a public spectacle of them all (Colossians 2:15). Jesus' crucifixion and resurrection stripped the devil of any authority he had to operate in power over us. Colossians says in the Amplified Bible:

> When you were dead in your sins and in the uncircumcision of your flesh (worldliness, manner of life), God made you alive together with Christ, having [freely] forgiven us all our sins, having canceled out the certificate of debt consisting of legal demands [which were in force] against us and which were hostile to us. And this certificate He has set aside *and* completely removed by nailing it to the cross. When He had disarmed the rulers and authorities [those supernatural forces of evil operating against us], He made a public example of them [exhibiting them as captives in His triumphal procession], having triumphed over them through the cross. (Colossians 2:13-15 AMP)

Satan is the father of lies and he is an expert at deception. In fact, he acts much like one of those creatures on the earth that will puff themselves up to appear bigger than they really are to intimidate predators, except he's the predator! He's a fake and his complete end is near. He is now and will always be the loser. And he knows it. He doesn't want you to know it… but now you do.

Please do not spend another moment intimidated by him. There is absolutely no reason for you to fear him. He is a bug under your feet.

WHO ARE WE?

I'm going to warn you right now; this is going to seem like a trick question: Who are you? We think that's an easy question but think about that for a moment. How would you answer?

Most of us would answer with what we do—our occupation, what roles we fill and perhaps how many children we have, but that's not really *who* we are at our core. In fact, if we define ourselves by our occupation and roles, our identity becomes muddled and we become uncertain of who we are when we perhaps lose our job, change careers and/or when our roles in life shift, for instance when our children grow up, start their own lives and become independent. It *can* cause mothers especially to go through an identity crisis when they are no longer needed by their children. It is much better to define ourselves by what won't change—by the eternal aspects of who we are. With that in mind, I might answer, "I am Barbara Jane, daughter of the most-high God, Jehovah, younger sibling to Jesus Christ of Nazareth, blessed and highly favored, called to encourage the Bride of Christ to walk in everything Christ died to give her—freedom, righteousness, and holiness." All who have surrendered their hearts to Jesus and accepted God's free gift of salvation can also claim their identity as a son or daughter of God. John 1:10-13 says:

> He was in the world, and the world was made through Him, and the world did not know Him. He came to His own, and His own did not receive Him. But as many as received Him, to them He gave the right to become children of God, to those who believe in His name: who were born, not of blood, nor of the will of the flesh, nor of the will of man, but of God.

As children of God, we have been re-born—born of the Spirit. In John 3, Nicodemus, a Pharisee, meets with Jesus in secret and tries to understand how one can be *born again*. Beginning in verse five, Jesus says to Nicodemus:

> "Most assuredly, I say to you, unless one is born of water and the Spirit, he cannot enter the kingdom of God. That which is born of the flesh is flesh, and that which is born of the Spirit is spirit. Do not marvel that I said to you, 'You must be born again.' The wind blows where it wishes, and you hear the sound of it, but cannot tell where it comes from and where it goes. So is everyone who is born of the Spirit." (John 3:5-8)

It's a bit of a mind bender, isn't it? By all appearances, nothing has changed, but that couldn't be further from the truth. Nicodemus struggled to understand it, and I think many of us do too.

When we are born in the natural, we are born of the flesh. Our flesh is formed, and our soul comes alive in the womb with the help of our Creator, but our spirit man inside is not alive to God; we are only flesh... completely and solely carnal. Because of the sin of Adam and Eve, every person born physically is born dead in spirit and disconnected from true life found only in God.[6] Our family is merely our natural family related by natural blood. But, when we surrender to Christ, a miracle takes place on the inside, in the invisible spiritual realm, and our spirit-man is re-born coming alive to God and connected eternally to His heart and Spirit. We become part of God's family connected by the blood of Jesus shed on our behalf. Second Corinthians 5:17 tells us that we are new creations in Christ—not creations that have been renovated or spruced-up but brand-new creations. The old is completely done away with and the new is here!

> So from now on we don't look at anyone the way the world does. At one time we looked at Christ in that way. But we don't anymore. When anyone lives in Christ, the new creation has come. The old is gone! The new is here! All this is from God. He brought us back to himself through Christ's death on the cross. And he has given us the task of bringing others back to him through Christ. (2 Cor. 5:16-18 NIRV)

Ephesians 2 also gives us great insight into how we have changed as children of God:

> Once you were dead because of your disobedience and your many sins. You used to live in sin, just like the rest of the world, obeying the devil—the commander of the powers in the unseen world. He is the spirit at work in the hearts of those who refuse to obey God. All of us used to live that way, following the passionate desires and inclinations of our sinful nature. By our very nature we were subject to God's anger, just like everyone else. But God is so rich in mercy, and he loved us so much, that even though we were dead because of our sins, he gave us life when he raised Christ from the dead. (It is only by God's grace that you have been saved!) For *he raised us from the dead along with Christ and seated us with him in the heavenly realms* because we are united with Christ Jesus. So God can point to us in all future ages as examples of the incredible wealth of his grace and kindness toward us, as shown in all he has done for us who are united with Christ Jesus.... For we are God's masterpiece. He has created us anew in Christ Jesus, so we can do the good things he planned for us long ago. (Ephesians 2:1-7; 10 NLT, emphasis added)

It never gets old reading about how God has transformed us spiritually! He has raised us up with Christ and seated us in heavenly places with Him. Jesus sits at the right-hand of God and this scripture passage is telling us that we sit there with Him. Our lives are hidden in Christ! We are His body. We are in heavenly places with Him—not physically of course, but spiritually speaking, we are. We are citizens of heaven (Philippians 3:20), Christ's ambassadors living on the earth re-presenting Him to the world (2nd Cor. 5:20). And in Christ, we have become the righteousness of God (2nd Cor. 5:21). We are a chosen generation, appointed, predestined to belong to Him, a royal priesthood, a holy nation, His own special people, bought at a price to belong to Him (1st Peter 2:9, 1st Cor. 6:20, Eph. 1:4-5).

The following is adapted from Neil T. Anderson's book, *Victory Over the Darkness*. In Christ, by His grace and mercy, we are:

- the salt of the earth (Matt. 5:13).
- the light of the world (Matt. 5:14).
- children of God (John 1:12).
- part of the true vine, a channel of Christ's life (John 15:1&5).
- Christ's friends (John 15:15).
- chosen and appointed by Christ to bear His fruit (John 15:16).
- slaves to righteousness (Romans 6:18).
- enslaved to God (Romans 6:22).
- sons and daughters of God; God is spiritually our Father (Romans 8:14-15; Galatians 3:26; 4:6).
- joint heirs with Christ, sharing in His inheritance with Him (Romans 8:17).

- temples of the Holy Spirit—dwelling places of God (1st Cor. 3:16; 6:19).
- united to the Lord and one spirit with Him (1st Cor. 6:17).
- members of Christ's body (1st Cor. 12:27; Eph. 5:30).
- reconciled to God and ministers of reconciliation (2nd Cor. 5:18-19).
- heirs of God (Gal. 4:6-7).
- saints (1st Cor. 1:2; Eph. 1:1; Phil. 1:1; Col. 1:2).
- prisoners of Christ (Eph. 3:1; 4:1).
- righteous and holy (Eph. 4:24).
- hidden with Christ in God (Col. 3:3).
- expressions of the life of Christ because He is our life (Col. 3:4).
- chosen of God, holy and dearly loved (Col. 3:12; 1st Thess. 1:4).
- sons and daughters of light and not of darkness (1st Thess. 5:5).
- holy partakers of a heavenly calling (Heb. 3:1).
- partakers of Christ; we share in His life (Heb. 3:14).
- God's living stones being built up in Christ as a spiritual house (1st Peter 2:5).
- aliens and strangers to this world in which we temporarily live (1st Peter 2:11 AMP).
- children of God who will resemble Him when He returns (1st John 3:2).
- complete in Christ (Col. 2:10).
- overcomers (1st John 5:4, "For every child of God defeats this evil world, and we achieve this victory through our faith." NLT).
- safe from harm—the devil cannot touch us (1st John 5:18, "We know that God's children do not make a practice of

sinning, for God's Son holds them securely, and the evil one cannot touch them." NLT).

Because we are now Christ's own possession, we also have access to His victory over the devil and according to Luke 10:19, He has given us authority in Him to overcome all the power of the devil. Luke 10:19 says:

> Behold, I give you the authority to trample on serpents and scorpions, and over all the power of the enemy, and nothing shall by any means hurt you.

I pray that you are encouraged by that amazing list of truths about you… in Christ. None of it is true because of what you have done. We cannot take any credit or glory. Instead, it is ALL true purely because of Christ's sacrifice for us. It is all God's doing.

Here's the mystery in it all. We actually don't walk it out perfectly yet, do we? *But* we can still claim it as true RIGHT NOW, because God says it is true RIGHT NOW. God gives us *everything* up front (because of His amazing grace). He credits our identity as being pure and holy just like Jesus BEFORE we are able to walk it out perfectly because He knows He is able to transform us into the image of His Son as we submit to Him. And He is already executing that plan in you and in me!

I choose to believe God's Word about me *despite* my periodic failures. What about you? Will you choose to believe it for yourself? God's Word is truth. Let's stand on it for ourselves and resist anything contrary to it. There is power in believing the truth about yourself and declaring it out loud. It empowers you and sets you up to behave like the favored daughter that you are.

Many Christians struggle with their behavior. They can't seem to get out of a pattern of sin. Sometimes deliverance is needed but sometimes it's simply a matter of renouncing the lies they've believed about their identity. If they believe that they are a *no-good loser*, they will act like a *no-good loser*. But if they renounce those self-deprecating thoughts and believe the truth instead, they will begin to behave like the daughter that they are. I find making the following declaration out loud over myself most helpful: "Because I am in Christ, I have been set free from the law of sin and death. It no longer has any more power over me. I am free to choose not to sin! I am free to choose holiness. I am free to do what is right."

Some Christians, after identifying with Christ in His death and resurrection, still believe they are "a sinner saved by grace." But this is not true! We've already been *spiritually* resurrected! This means we are saints. No longer sinners. Yes, we've been saved by grace. And yes, sometimes the flesh that is supposed to be dead tries to rise up again, but "sinner" is no longer our identity. Identifying the lies that we believe about ourselves and replacing them with truth sets us free to live victoriously.

> It is for freedom that Christ has set us free. Stand firm, then, and do not let yourselves be burdened again by a yoke of slavery (to the law or a need to be perfect in your own strength). (Gal. 5:1a NIV, brackets added)

> You who are trying to be justified by the law have been alienated from Christ; you have fallen away from grace. For through the Spirit we eagerly await *by faith* the righteousness for which we hope. (Gal. 5:4-5 NIV, emphasis added)

Praise the Lord.

Lastly, our struggle with the enemy is not a power struggle. We are on the same team with Jesus—God's team—so there is no contest. Satan doesn't have a chance. No...

Our struggle against the devil is not about power; it's about truth and our boldness and willingness to stand on it.

> John 8:32 says, "And you shall know the truth, and the truth shall make you free."

Rise up, daughter of God! It is time to stop allowing the enemy to lie to you and push you around. God is backing you up. Your Father is right behind you enforcing His victory through you.

---

[6]Genesis 2:16-17, "And the LORD God commanded the man, "You are free to eat from any tree in the garden; but you must not eat from the tree of the knowledge of good and evil, for when you eat from it you will certainly die" (NIV).

3

HOW'S YOUR HEART?

> Keep your heart with all diligence, for out of it spring the issues of life. (Proverbs 4:23) Watch over your heart with all diligence, for from it *flow* the springs of life. (Proverbs 4:23 AMP) Above all else, guard your heart, for everything you do flows from it. (Proverbs 4:23 NIV)

The heart. According to all three translations above, out of it "*spring the issues of life*," from it "*flow the springs of life*," and "*everything you do flows from it.*" There are subtle differences in each statement. The NKJV says the *"issues"* of life come out of the heart; the word *"issues"* usually refers to something negative or challenging. The AMP says the *"springs"* of life come out of the heart, which is more positive. The NIV says that our behavior—*everything* we do—is determined by the heart. And the NLT says, "*it determines the course of your life.*" Wow. The condition of our heart is very important.

Let's also consider Luke 6:45 which says the following:

> A good man out of the good treasure of his heart brings forth good; and an evil man out of the evil

> treasure of his heart brings forth evil. For out of the abundance of the heart his mouth speaks.

What we store up in our heart matters for multiple reasons, one of which is, our mouth will inadvertently leak what is there. If you allow someone to talk long enough, their words will eventually expose their heart; they will only be able to filter their words for so long.

"*The heart is our barometer.*" These are the words I heard in my spirit just now. So, let's consider this further. According to Bing.com, a barometer is "an instrument measuring atmospheric pressure, used especially in forecasting the weather and determining altitude." The heart determines the course of our life and just like a barometer, it reads the atmosphere we are in, gives us discernment, and determines the weather we will experience around us in life; if we have anger and hate in our heart, we set ourselves up for stormy weather. Lastly, the heart determines the altitude we can rise to in the Lord—the level of heaven we experience here on earth. Our heart is a vital piece of us, required to navigate life and experience God through the Holy Spirit. Without it and its sensitivity, we are just living carnally going through the motions.

So, how's your heart?

Multiple times throughout this book I will say, "*engage your heart,*" or "*bring your heart into agreement*" with what you're praying. We can't function spiritually with just our head; nothing is accomplished spiritually unless we engage our heart with what we're doing, saying, believing, and having faith for. In fact, faith, comes from the heart. Faith does not exist apart from our heart. Romans 10:9-10 says the following:

> If you openly declare that Jesus is Lord and *believe in your heart* that God raised him from the dead, you will be saved. For it is by *believing in your heart that you are made right with God*, and it is by openly declaring your faith that you are saved. (NLT, italics added)

We need to *believe in our heart* to be made right with God. This means we must know what is in our heart, and we must purposely engage our heart to have true faith. Faith is not just lip service or mental assent to the gospel. For some, this is an issue. And you already know who you are. So, what's the issue?

Some will say, "Well, I don't know how to bring my heart into agreement." "I feel like my head and my heart are not connected." "I know I believe in my head, but I have no idea if I believe in my heart." "How can I tell if my heart is engaged?" If you're saying these things, you probably struggle to identify your feelings. Perhaps your heart feels numb.

"Guard your heart," "Keep your heart," "Watch over your heart," means to be aware of what you're allowing into your heart and what you're allowing to stay there. But to do this, with the help of the Holy Spirit, we need to be able to discern or evaluate our own heart—the seat of our emotions, feelings, affections, and attitudes. Many readers cannot do that. So, we must settle this matter before we go any further.

When I was seventeen, I went through a bad breakup. It was my first serious relationship and my heart was crushed. To add insult to injury, he was told lies about me to make him believe I had cheated on him, so, he was horribly aggressive toward me after the breakup. Prior to our breakup, I thought perhaps we would get married one day, but almost overnight my perceived utopia imploded. I went from mountaintop bliss to being absolutely crushed in just a few days. It was a prime situation for me to decide that life was too painful, and I should just shut my heart down to protect it. I was in agony, and I could have decided it was too much to bear. Thankfully, I had been trained from a young age to trust God and run to Him when I was in need so that is what I did. Father, God, was my safe place. Unfortunately, few people have had this.

Everyone has had situations in life that have been difficult to bear emotionally; some have had situations that were impossible and didn't have a safe place to run for cover. Some people have even been in chronic unbearable situations; it wasn't just a few situations here and there. It was everyday life. In these cases, we need a coping mechanism, don't we? We need to survive.

One way to survive is to create a tough exterior, be strong, and shut the emotions down—don't let anything or anyone in—operate from logic, common sense, and mental capacity only. You may have done this, and it probably has served you. It may have kept you safe and able to function. But now, it has become a hindrance because as stated at the beginning of this chapter, we absolutely *need* to *feel* to connect, in the Spirit, with God. Feeling is not an option; feeling is necessary. And the ability to feel is crucial for our healing from all the junk we are tackling in this book. In chapter 6, *The Pit of Pits*, I will ask you to talk to God and tell Him how certain situations made you feel. The answer, *"I don't know,"* is not going to get you free. We need to *feel* all the feels and confess them to God. Transparency and authenticity are the gateway to healing.

Perhaps there was a moment when you said, "That's it. I'm done feeling. It's too painful. I don't know how to process this. It's not safe, so I'm *escaping* by shutting down. I decide not to care about anything or anyone anymore," and the devil said, "Great!" and he happily anesthetized your heart. You put up a wall, and the devil put it to sleep. But now, it's time to wake up! It's time to break the wall down. It's time to stop trying to hold it together, stop trying to control yourself, stop avoiding, stop hiding and stop "being strong" and breakdown. Break *down* in order to break *through*.

All the emotions you've had stored away in the hidden caverns of your heart need to be exposed, felt and let go. We do this by first deciding to trust God again. You might be saying, "But I don't think I could handle that much pain all at once; it might kill me." Thankfully...

God knows what you can handle and will only allow the tap of your emotions to open so far at any given moment.

I don't know if you knew God when you decided to shut down, but let me ask you this, "Are you angry at God for allowing the unjust treatment you have suffered—for allowing the difficulty you have had to face in life?" If so, I get it. It's confusing trying to reconcile in your head why an all-powerful God *seemingly* didn't protect you, but *that* is an argument the enemy puts in our head so we will blame God. We discuss *blaming God* in depth in the chapter, *The Pit of Pits*, so for now, let me just say that God chose at the very beginning of time to limit what He could do by giving us free-will.

God does not and cannot control people like puppets.

Everyone has the final choice as to whether they will act out in sin or not. So, the people that did not treat you properly were making choices that did not honor God; as a result, God's heart grieved for you. But your mistreatment or adversity was not God's plan, nor however, did it surprise Him; He knew it was coming, and He already had a plan to restore and heal your heart; this is why you hold this book in your hands right now. Your healing is imminent. However, your healing depends on your willingness to submit to God and trust Him again.

If you need to scream, "God!!! Why did you not protect me!!" Do it. If you need to scream, "God!! Where were you?!!!" Do it. He can handle your emotions and your pain. He can handle your true feelings.

But let Him answer you and show you the truth.

Be willing to hear Him out.

Be willing to see what He shows you.

Confess your anger toward Him. Don't try to hide it or diminish it. "God!!! I'm angry!" "I feel betrayed!" "I trusted You, and You weren't there for me." "I don't understand!!" This is what true relationship is about... being honest. Being vulnerable. Being transparent. God cannot help us if we refuse to admit our true feelings—if we simply try and say the *right* thing, feel the *right* thing, pray the *right* thing to avoid accountability. We need correction, friends. We need God to show us the truth and eliminate the lies and the accusations against Him that hide in our heart.

Consider Job. He was honest. Though he wrongly accused God of being unjust, he was honest, and because of that, he was restored through repentance. In Job 30:16-22, Job says the following:

> "And now my life seeps away. Depression haunts my days. At night my bones are filled with pain, which gnaws at me relentlessly. With a strong hand, God grabs my shirt. He grips me by the collar of my coat. He has thrown me into the mud. I'm nothing more than dust and ashes. "I cry to you, O God, but you don't answer. I stand before you, but you don't even look. *You have become cruel toward me. You use your power to persecute me. You throw me into the whirlwind and destroy me in the storm.* (NLT, italics added)

Those are some hefty accusations against God. Unfortunately, Job's pain gives him a distorted view of God and what He was doing. Thankfully, a man named Elihu righteously confronts Job in his sin and defends God in chapters 32-37. God finally speaks to Job directly in chapter 38 bringing him much needed correction. In fact, the Lord rebukes him for FOUR long chapters. Finally, in Job 42:2-6, Job repents which opens the door for God to accept him again and restore him.

> "I know that you can do all things; no purpose of yours can be thwarted. You asked, 'Who is this that obscures my plans without knowledge?' Surely I spoke of things I did not understand, things too wonderful for me to know. "You said, 'Listen now, and I will speak; I will question you, and you shall answer me.' My ears had heard of you but now my eyes have seen you. Therefore I despise myself and repent in dust and ashes." (Job 42:2-6 NIV)

When we are willing to be honest with the Lord, allow Him to correct us, and repent for our misunderstandings, He restores to us all that was lost with even more than we had before.

Job had to repent for pride and accusing God of being unjust. If we've been angry at God and blamed Him for our adversity, we also need to repent. We also need to repent for shutting our heart down, for turning off and numbing our feelings.

Pray with me friends:

> "Lord, God, I confess to You today that I shut my heart down—that I built a wall around my heart, created a tough exterior, and decided not to allow anything or anyone to hurt me anymore. I went into self-protection mode, hard-heartedness and cold-heartedness. I decided to stop caring about others. I decided You, God, were not faithful to protect me so I took that role onto myself. I thought I could do a better job at protecting myself. I was wrong and I have been prideful. I repent. Please forgive me, God. I confess that I have been bitter toward You and others. I repent. Please forgive me.
>
> I choose to forgive myself for my error and I choose to forgive all those who have hurt me, including... *[if there is someone that comes to mind who may be the one who caused you to shut down, forgive them here specifically]*.
>
> According to Your Word God, I thank You for Your forgiveness and I receive it in fullness now. Cleanse me from all unrighteousness. Heal the wounds of my heart, God, restore Your truth to my mind. Make me new.
>
> I renounce hard-heartedness and cold-heartedness. And I renounce pride, bitterness, and self-protection.

I receive now the new heart of flesh You have for me (according to Ezekiel 11:19), and I give You the hard-heart I created... the heart of stone which I have no more use for, that I no longer need nor want. *[See yourself giving your heart of stone to Jesus.]* I give it to You, God. Crush it. Break it. Smash it to pieces.

Cold-heartedness and hard-heartedness, leave me now in Jesus' name. Self-protection, leave me now in Jesus' name. Bitterness, leave me now, in Jesus' name.

I speak to my heart of flesh and I say, "Come alive in me now, in Jesus' name." I receive it from You, God. I receive it now. I agree with God and say, "Heart of flesh, beat with a new rhythm. Beat with new life and new purpose. Beat with the love of God AND the love of people." I speak to myself and I say, "Come alive! Come alive! In Jesus' name. Come out of the hidden place. Come out of darkness and captivity, in Jesus' name."

Thank You, Jesus! Thank You for Your faithfulness. Restore to me the joy of Your salvation. Restore to me peace in my inner man. Restore to me healthy emotional balance, identification, and expression. Help me to let You in as well as the right people and help me not to bury my feelings but let them out in a godly way. Put Your hedge of protection around my heart and give me Your wisdom and discernment according to Your will. Give me courage to put healthy boundaries in place so I am not taken advantage of by others.

> Holy Spirit, fill me afresh in this place of surrender. Saturate me in Your peace and power. May Your presence be in me and rest on me as I set myself apart for You, in Jesus' name."

And I declare over you a breaking out of old patterns... a breaking out of old cycles and a propelling forward into the new. The Lord has placed His holy defibrillator on you bringing you back to life... back to His life in you. Receive it now! I declare the Holy Spirit hovering over you, brooding, surrounding, infiltrating wounded places and bringing His healing balm... His healing oil and liquid love. You will no longer operate from dead, wounded places but from a heart fully alive in Christ, feeling, beating, loving, and forgiving appropriately. All residue from self-protection, apathy, withdrawal, numbness, and the fear of being hurt goes now, in Jesus' name. Loose my sister now, in Jesus' name! Shove off in Jesus' name. You no longer belong here. She belongs to Jesus. She is a daughter of the King. Chosen. Separated. Redeemed. Resurrected. Made whole. Covered. Accepted. Beloved.

Receive it. Believe it. Feel it.

Soak in it.

Play your favorite worship song and literally soak in His presence just to solidify and bring God's work in you to completion.

We seal what God has done, in Jesus' name. Nothing shall be stolen or nullified. Nothing shall be twisted or distorted, in Jesus' name. What has been made holy shall remain. Hallelujah.

Step into the increase sis. Allow God to raise your faith to new levels. Let's go.

4

SHAME

"Fear not; you will no longer live in shame. Don't be afraid; there is no more disgrace for you. *You will no longer remember the shame of your youth* and the sorrows of widowhood.
(Isaiah 54:4 NLT, italics added)

"*You will no longer remember the shame of your youth...*" Such a great promise! When we allow the Lord to be our all in all... to be our Healer by opening our heart to Him and letting our shame be exposed to Him, He will remove it along with the pain associated with it. He will heal the wounds of our heart.

We have established some foundational truth in the first few chapters and allowed God to bring us back to life, but now we begin to tackle the different contributing factors to sexual dysfunction. The fruit of sexual dysfunction is unrelenting sexual temptation, intrusive sexual thoughts and/or dreams, frigidity or an overactive sex drive, but the roots of the problem are unclean spirits which have gained access to us through open spiritual doors in our life. Open doors could be wounds of the heart, past trauma, sin committed against us, our own sin, or generational sin (iniquity). In this chapter, we will deal with the lynchpin of the whole mess: shame. Shame is what holds it all together. Shame is what locks the prison door. Shame is what keeps us in the dark, entrenched in a cycle of sexual temptation and sin… an easy target for the devil.

Is there anything in your youth that you feel shame over? For some of us, the shame is buried alive and we have vowed never to talk about it with anyone—to never admit *that* indiscretion ever happened. Some of us think we can just leave it and forget about it and somehow it won't affect us. But it does. For some the shame is so heavy they have had to seal and shut their whole heart and emotions down to keep it hidden. And we believe that if our secret is ever exposed, we will never recover. I believed that myself for a long time.

Shame is especially strong about events that have taken place in our childhood—the things we participated in willingly which perhaps we didn't realize were wrong or the things that we didn't want to participate in but couldn't get out of because of a sense of powerlessness and confusion.

I kept a secret for a long time. But in my thirties, I found myself in a Bible study with a group of older women whom I looked up to. As we chatted, I found myself thinking about a childhood sexual event that I participated in with a friend.

My friend and I were probably seven years old or so. At the time, I didn't know much about sexual things—only that one day I was going to have to do stuff, like kiss boys, and I didn't know how. That made me nervous. So, my friend and I "practiced" with one another. At least that was my thinking process; that is what I thought we were doing. I had no idea I wasn't supposed to do these things with another girl. But as I got older and realized my mistake, the shame hit hard. I didn't want anyone to know.

Anyhow, I sat with this group of women that morning, casually sipping on tea, and the Holy Spirit put His finger on this event in my childhood and told me it was time to bring it into the light. My heart just about beat out of my chest! I didn't want to admit my sin to them. I didn't want to be exposed. I was afraid of what they would think of me. And it was very embarrassing. The shame was very strong; I stuttered as I tried to speak. It wouldn't come out! I physically could not say it. But I pushed and my body literally shook; my secret held me in chains. They prayed in tongues as I continued to push through and eventually, I got it out.

The lovely woman beside me said, "Oh! I did that too!" (lol)

"You did!?"

I couldn't believe it. She wasn't all bound up in shame and fear! *So, why was I*?!

Thankfully, as soon as I got it out into the open, the shame broke. We laughed about it and I could see how ridiculous it was to be so ashamed of something I had done, *as an innocent child*, without any awareness of it being wrong.

Here's another story for you: Several years ago, I had been actively trying to eliminate perverted demonic interference in my mind and dreams through prayer, repentance, and purposely not watching any movies or shows with explicit sexual scenes. It was good, and I was gaining victory, until one night I had a sexual dream with a man from my community whom I used to know. It was disturbing. And in the dream, I did not want to be in that situation, but I did not physically resist what was happening. In the dream, I felt grief in my heart. In the middle of our indiscretion, Father God, came around the corner upon the scene. I saw Him, then everything in the dream... the man... our activity... all of it, just dissipated. I went to Father God, and I literally *melted* into Him and became part of Him. His love received me. There was no gasp or, "I can't believe you were doing *that*!" There was no shame. There was no shock in His eyes. Just perfect love. And peace. It was what my heart needed, and it brought great healing to the shame I had felt in the past from something my earthly father saw. So, we can be rest assured that anything we go to our heavenly Father with, He will not shame us for. He will only accept us and love us in the greatest possible way—no strings attached. I'm so grateful.

Let's continue to look at Isaiah 54 from verse five and forward.

> For your Creator will be your husband; the LORD of Heaven's Armies is his name! He is your Redeemer, the Holy One of Israel, the God of all the earth. For the LORD has called you back from your grief—as though you were a young wife abandoned by her husband," says your God. (Isaiah 54:5-6 NLT)

Isaiah 54 is written to and about the city of Jerusalem and its inhabitants, but God's heart is clearly identified for His people, which includes us. We are grafted into the people of God.[7] The Lord has called us back out of grief and shame, into His healing and restoration. But it begins with our willingness to open our heart and confess what is buried there, to God.

Let's look at Psalms 18. It is long but I believe it is important.

> I love you, LORD; you are my strength. The LORD is my rock, my fortress, and my savior; my God is my rock, in whom I find protection. He is my shield, the power that saves me, and my place of safety. I called on the LORD, who was worthy of praise, and he saved me from my enemies. The

ropes of death entangled me; floods of destruction swept over me. The grave wrapped its ropes around me; death laid a trap in my path. But in my distress I cried out to the LORD; yes, I prayed to my God for help. He heard me from his sanctuary; my cry to him reached his ears. Then the earth quaked and trembled. The foundations of the mountains shook; they quaked because of his anger. Smoke poured from his nostrils; fierce flames leaped from his mouth. Glowing coals blazed forth from him. He opened the heavens and came down; dark storm clouds were beneath his feet. Mounted on a mighty angelic being, he flew, soaring on the wings of the wind. He shrouded himself in darkness, veiling his approach with dark rain clouds. Thick clouds shielded the brightness around him and rained down hail and burning coals. The LORD thundered from heaven; the voice of the Most High resounded amid the hail and burning coals. He shot his arrows and scattered his enemies; great bolts of lightning flashed, and they were confused. Then at your command, O LORD, at the blast of your breath, the bottom of the sea could be seen, and the foundations of the earth were laid bare. He reached down from heaven and rescued me; he drew me out of deep waters. He rescued me from my powerful enemies, from those who hated me and were too strong for me. They attacked me at a moment when I was in distress, but the LORD supported me.

He led me to a place of safety; *he rescued me because he delights in me.*

27You rescue the humble, but you humiliate the proud. You light a lamp for me. The LORD, my

God, lights up my darkness. In your strength I can crush an army; with my God I can scale any wall. God's way is perfect. All the LORD's promises prove true. He is a shield for all who look to him for protection. For who is God except the LORD? Who but our God is a solid rock? God arms me with strength, and he makes my way perfect. He makes me as surefooted as a deer, enabling me to stand on mountain heights. He trains my hands for battle; he strengthens my arm to draw a bronze bow. You have given me your shield of victory. Your right hand supports me; your help has made me great. You have made a wide path for my feet to keep them from slipping. I chased my enemies and caught them; I did not stop until they were conquered. I struck them down so they could not get up; they fell beneath my feet. You have armed me with strength for the battle; you have subdued my enemies under my feet. You placed my foot on their necks. I have destroyed all who hated me. They called for help, but no one came to their rescue. They even cried to the LORD, but he refused to answer. I ground them as fine as dust in the wind. I swept them into the gutter like dirt. You gave me victory over my accusers. You appointed me ruler over nations; people I don't even know now serve me. As soon as they hear of me, they submit; foreign nations cringe before me. They all lose their courage and come trembling from their strongholds. The LORD lives! Praise to my Rock! May the God of my salvation be exalted! He is the God who pays back those who harm me; he subdues the nations under me and rescues me from my enemies. You hold me safe beyond the reach of my enemies; you save me from violent opponents.

> For this, O LORD, I will praise you among the nations; I will sing praises to your name. You give great victories to your king; you show unfailing love to your anointed, to David and all his descendants forever. (Psalms 18:1-19, 27-50 NLT, italics added for emphasis)

Lately, the Lord has been saying to me, "Remember Who I Am!" Psalms 18 gives us a great idea of Who God is, as King David sings the praises of the One who has just powerfully rescued him from his foes. See how David cries out to God for rescue and see how utterly desperate he was. David was in deep trouble! "The grave wrapped its ropes around" him. "Death laid a trap" in his path. His enemies were hunting him to kill him. His very life hung in the balance. And God came down from heaven cloaked in the clouds to smite David's enemies. See God's fierce anger against the ones coming against David, his servant. God is a consuming fire! He is our ferocious Defender.

David's battle was against people—against Saul, and Saul's men. Our battle is NOT against flesh and blood but against evil rulers, authorities in the unseen realm, and powers of darkness but God is just as ferocious on our behalf as He was for David. God comes through for us in the same way. God's character is the same yesterday, today, and forever. His identity as Fierce Protector and Defender has not changed. God is still a Fierce Protector and Defender. He is OUR Fierce Protector and Defender. And He is a CONSUMING FIRE against the powers of the unseen realm that try to keep us in chains. He is a CONSUMING FIRE against shame! And He enables you to be His warrior against shame as well.

Notice these verses again:

> God arms me with strength, and he makes my way perfect. He makes me as surefooted as a deer, enabling me to stand on mountain heights. He trains my hands for battle; he strengthens my arm to draw a bronze bow. You have given me your shield of victory. Your right hand supports me; your help has made me great. You have made a wide path for my feet to keep them from slipping. I chased my enemies and caught them; I did not stop until they were conquered. I struck them down so they could not get up; they fell beneath my feet. You have armed me with strength for the battle; you have subdued my enemies under my feet. You placed my foot on their necks. I have destroyed all who hated me. (Psalms 18:32-40 NLT)

The battle belongs to the Lord but that doesn't mean we sit on our hands. It means we partner with Him and He strengthens us to do what we need to do to win the battle. It means we do our part and we pursue our enemies to take them out.

In 1 Samuel 30 David and his men come back to their home-base in Ziklag only to find that the Amalekites had burned their community to the ground and taken all their wives and children captive. David inquired of the Lord, "Shall I pursue this troop? Shall I overtake them?" And God answered David, "Pursue, for you shall surely overtake them and without fail recover all" (1 Samuel 30:8). God says to *you* today, "Pursue, overtake and recover all!" Pursue your enemy today. Overtake shame and recover all—recover your dignity, your heart, and your emotions. Recover your strength, your courage and your grit to push through the challenge in front of you so by the end, you can say, "I am healed and I am whole! Lust and twisted perceptions, ideas, and desires have no hold on me, in Jesus' name!"

PRAYER

Pray this out loud: "Lord God, I repent for partnering with shame and believing the lies it propagates. Please forgive me. I renounce the lie that I will be judged by others, and I renounce the lie that I am an awful person and won't be forgiven—that what I've done is too terrible even for God to forgive. I renounce the lie that I will be rejected when someone finds out what I've done/was done to me. I renounce the lie that I should be ashamed of myself, and I break the power of the word curse, "shame on you." I choose to forgive myself for partnering with shame and believing lies. I receive your forgiveness, God. Thank you."

Declare this out loud: "I choose right now to come out of agreement with shame and its lies. I renounce shame now, in Jesus' name. And I completely divorce myself from it, in Jesus' name. Amen."

FEAR

We will also need to come out of agreement with fear to move forward. Let's brainstorm what we might be afraid of when revealing our secret. We could be afraid of exposure, more shame, rejection, blame, judgement, peoples' opinions, reprimand, reproof, loss of control over what people think of us, not being liked, not being accepted, not being loved, mockery, and invalidation. We may even be afraid of being charged criminally if we were the perpetrator in abuse. All these fears can be put into God's capable hands, and we can ask God to be in control of every outcome—to vindicate us. "For God has not given us a spirit of fear, but of power and of love and of a sound mind" (2nd Timothy 1:7).

PRAYER

> Pray this out loud: "Lord God, I repent for partnering with fear, particularly the fear of exposure, fear of more shame, rejection, blame, judgement, peoples' opinions, reprimand, reproof, loss of control over what people think of me, the fear of not being liked, accepted or loved, the fear of mockery, and the fear of invalidation (and the fear of criminal charges if applicable). Please forgive me, God. Thank You. According to 1st John 1:9, I receive Your forgiveness and cleansing now, in Jesus' name."
>
> Declare this out loud: "I choose right now to come out of agreement with all fear, in Jesus' name. I bind and renounce all fear that has been keeping me from moving forward and I completely divorce myself from it, because I know that my God has not given me a spirit of fear, but of power, love and a sound mind. In Jesus' name, amen."

Now, ask the Holy Spirit, "Who do You want me to talk to about this?" And let Him bring someone to your mind. Shame breaks when you bring what is connected to it into the light. Remember when I told you that I had to tell my ladies' group about my indiscretion as a child? I had to battle shame in order to get it out of my mouth. My body literally trembled as I tried to speak. Shame did not want me to confess it. That's because shame loses its grip on us when we tell someone our secret. If the Lord doesn't show you someone right away, wait on Him and trust Him to lead you. Perhaps He will show you as you go about your day.

Perhaps He will prompt your heart in the moment when you're with someone.

Secrets hold us in chains. Your first act of freedom as you work through this book is to find a trustworthy friend, counsellor, therapist, or pastor to confess your secret to and pray with. And right now, I break the power of shame over you! And I break the power of fear, in Jesus' name. Fear of exposure, fear of judgement, fear of peoples' opinions, fear of rejection, fear of reprimand, fear of reproof, fear of more shame, I bind now and break its power over you, in Jesus' name. You are a daughter of the King and will not live in shame any longer. You will rise and become all God created you to be. You will rise and open your heart again to feel, to love, to have compassion, to cry, and to be used in ministry as the Lord leads. You will no longer be a victim but an OVERCOMER in His name! You will not sit in a pit but rise and soar on His wings of love and freedom. Jesus suffered and died so you could be victorious with Him. Now rise! Get up. Pray. Confess. Repent. Renounce. Declare who you are in Him. You are forgiven. You are made whole. You are a brand-new creation! The old is gone and the new has come. You are no longer a sinner, but a saint saved by the grace and mercy of God. You are mighty in God. Wield your sword! And take your enemies down in His might and in His truth.

---

[7] Romans 11:17, "But some of these branches from Abraham's tree—some of the people of Israel—have been broken off. And you Gentiles, who were branches from a wild olive tree, have been grafted in. So now you also receive the blessing God has promised Abraham and his children, sharing in the rich nourishment from the root of God's special olive tree." (NLT)

5

SQUARE ONE

If we confess our sins, he is faithful and just to forgive us *our* sins and to cleanse us from all unrighteousness. (1 John 1:9)

As I begin this chapter and start to "get down to brass tacks," I sense the compassion of the Lord very strongly. And I sense Him reminding us, "For we do not have a High Priest who cannot sympathize with our weaknesses, but was in all points tempted as we are…" (Hebrews 4:15). He knows we are dust. He knows our weaknesses well. Praise God. He does not condemn us or sit in judgement against us. Nor does He say, "Shame on you." No! No. A thousand times, no. That is not His heart. *That* voice is the enemy. Make sure you're not agreeing with shame again.

To be very honest with you, this book feels like a massive mountain to climb, and I don't know how to climb it. Where do we start? How do I proceed to make the best progress? What do we consider first? I feel like we wouldn't be struggling with anything related to sexuality if it weren't for something that happened *to* us in our earlier years—something done to us which was completely out of our control and understanding. I believe that most, if not all of us, can track dysfunction in sexuality right back to childhood. I'm certain of it. However, let's continue with us and how we have partnered with dysfunction. Let's work our way backwards from now to then. Okay? I feel like this may be the easy part.

In summary, if we do not have victory in the area of sexuality, meaning we feel somehow stuck in poor choices or something ungodly, whether it be deviant sexual desire, thoughts we can't control, or a complete lack of interest, we must tackle what is fueling the dysfunction. Here is a more detailed list of things to consider:

- our own sexual sin;
- the soul-ties that have been formed through sex;
- sexual abuse we have suffered and the related trauma, fear, unforgiveness, anger, hate, bitterness, judgements and vows;
- sexual molestation we have suffered and the related trauma, fear, unforgiveness, anger, hate, bitterness, judgements, and vows;
- our ancestor's sexual sin and trauma that has carried forward to us;
- PLUS, all *sexually charged*, *embarrassing* situations that have caused shame and perhaps bitter judgements against others, no matter how insignificant we think it was. (I have a prime example I will share later.)

Here's the tricky part: What actually falls into the category of sin where sex is concerned? Some sexual sin is obvious, and some isn't; some is identified outright in the Bible, and some isn't. For instance, fornication is clearly identified in the Bible as a sin. Fornication is sex before marriage. But is that just intercourse or does fornication include ALL sexual activity? I believe it includes all sexual activity. (Basically, in my opinion, if you can't do it in front of your father, you shouldn't be doing it.) We must confess and repent for fornication if we want to be forgiven and cleansed and have the door of "willful sin" closed, so the enemy can't touch us. This goes for all other sexual sins as well. But what are those sexual sins? What exactly is "sexual immorality?" What does it include?

The truth is, around the topic of sexuality, there is a lot of confusion. What do we need to confess in this area and what can we continue to enjoy? The Bible is not super clear about *some stuff,* and it has left some things ambiguous. Much of the confusion is caused by our flesh having some really strong opinions (in this area) because *it* has the most to lose—namely the pleasure it has enjoyed in the past.

You might be surprised at the confusion some are in. Some are so confused they don't think it's a big deal to view pornography, even though in Matthew 5:27-28 Jesus says the following:

> "You have heard that it was said to those of old, 'You shall not commit adultery.' But I say to you that whoever looks at a woman to lust for her has already committed adultery with her in his heart."

Married people who view pornography are committing adultery in their heart. If that is true, then unmarried people who view pornography are committing fornication in their heart. According to scripture, lusting after someone for sex is equivalent to actually doing it.

Additionally, some people forget that pornographic pictures and movies use real people. Just because we don't know them personally doesn't mean they aren't real or that we shouldn't care about them. Very often those people are doing what they are doing against their will. They are trapped in prostitution or human trafficking situations. They are on drugs and they are addicted. No one chooses that kind of degrading life nor wants to be there.

Lord, give us clarity!

I could sit here and rattle off all the things that I am convicted don't fit into God's original plan for sex, and tell you to repent, but if *you* are not convicted by the Holy Spirit about the same things, your confession is useless; your confession is not *heart-felt.* You must confess and repent for what *you* are convicted about. Now I know that most people reading these words know how to confess their sin and know how to repent. So, if that's you, great!! You've probably already done it. But surprisingly, some people who have even been in the church a long time, don't realize that they need to go to God in prayer and repent for their sin. Not sure why, but it's true.

So, the first category of things that will keep us stuck in bondage is the sin we have committed which we have not taken to the Lord in confession and repentance. What is repentance? Repentance is *not* only feeling bad for what you have done; naturally when we are convicted by the Holy Spirit, we are remorseful. But repentance more fully understood is an active decision to stop what you are doing and turn around, bringing your heart to God in confession and asking for forgiveness. It includes remorse but it also includes a revelation of guilt that requires cleansing and an active decision to do better.

APPLICATION

Your first task, because this book isn't just about acquiring information but about *applying* what we are learning and getting free, is to make a list of ALL the partners you have had outside of marriage if any, and all the sexual behaviors you have *voluntarily* been a part of that are outside of standard sexual practice. And pray about it all. Ask the Holy Spirit to convict your heart about anything that was not godly. Here are a few Bible passages you can read, in addition, to help you discern:

- 1 Corinthians 5:1-11, 6:9-20, 7:1-9
- Ephesians 5:1-12
- 1 Timothy 1:8-11
- Romans 1:20-32, 13:11-14
- 1 Thessalonians 4:3-8
- Galatians 5:16-26
- Colossians 3:5-17
- Mark 7:20-23
- Hebrews 13:4
- 1 Peter 2:11-12
- Jude 1:7
- Leviticus 18

I pray that you would have ears to hear what the Spirit is saying. Do not compromise. I know it's tempting. Your flesh and the devil are warring against you but press in my friend. Your freedom depends on it. Notice the terms "lewdness" and "uncleanness;" ask the Holy Spirit the following:

1. "What is lewdness?"
2. "What do You consider lewd, Lord?"
3. "Are there any sexual acts that You consider unclean?"

Read the passages above in a few different translations. Look up commentaries online to learn more. Seek the Lord!

PRAYER

> "Father, forgive me for participating in the following sexual sin: (list everything you are convicted to confess.)
>
> I repent. I choose to turn away from all these behaviors now. Forgive me, God, for using my body as an instrument of unrighteousness. I choose to forgive myself and I choose to forgive (name every partner) for participating with me."

If you felt pressured into it:

> "I choose to forgive (name your partner) for pressuring me into it and/or taking advantage of me."
>
> "Lord, I receive Your forgiveness and Your cleansing in its fullness according to 1st John 1:9. Lord, I ask You now to heal the wounds of my heart that caused me to seek out this type of attention and affection and heal the wounds that were created because of this sin. Send the power of Your Holy Spirit and pour out Your healing oil over my heart. I receive it now. Thank You for Your faithfulness and Your mercy over my life.
>
> I renounce (name all the sins you confessed), in Jesus' name.
>
> Lord, if there is something else I need to confess and renounce, please show me what that is."

Wait on the Lord for a few minutes. You could pray in tongues to gain clarity in the Spirit. If He shows you something, confess and renounce it.

> "Thank You, Jesus. Fill me up, Lord. Baptize be afresh in Your Spirit, in Your name. Amen"

That's a great start to this challenging journey. Good job.

Next, we are going to talk about the soul-ties that are created when we have intercourse and become one with others, along with the need to break them and how.

SOUL-TIES

A soul-tie is a deep emotional attachment with another person, a pet or even a thing that you have come to depend on to derive purpose, value or comfort. This connection can be godly in certain situations but is very often ungodly.

A soul-tie can be made a few different ways. They primarily are made through sexual intercourse as those who have sex become "one flesh." This is why we are only supposed to have sex with our spouse. We get ourselves into bad situations when we become "one flesh" with multiple people; the dysfunction in their flesh can transfer to ours.

To give you a complete understanding, soul-ties can also be made through relying too heavily on someone else (a mother for instance) or even some*thing* to meet our emotional needs, specifically for safety, love, worth, and purpose. Lastly, soul-ties can be made through the emotional entanglement that comes with fearing someone or hating someone.

In some instances, soul-ties can be godly, such as in a *healthy* marriage relationship between a husband and wife, and in *healthy* parent-child relationships, however, in each instance, soul-ties can easily develop ungodly portions that don't serve us, don't glorify God, and give the enemy a foothold in our lives. This is due to wounds we may have accumulated in childhood possibly due to mistreatment. Examples of this are the following: a husband trying to control his wife; abuse in marriage; elevating the opinion or acceptance of your spouse above God's opinion or acceptance; an insecure parent not allowing their child to grow up, becoming independent; or a child remaining emotionally immature not wanting to grow up but relying on their parent after what is appropriate.

God's design was for each person to connect with Him and rely on Him as their main *source* of love, acceptance, and self-worth (think of the original garden, the Garden of Eden, and how Adam and Eve were secure in their identity because of their relationship with God the Father). So, if we look to and *depend* on someone else to love us, validate us, make us worthy, comfort us, and keep us safe, we end up trying to derive our value and security from another person. In so doing, we end up creating a connection of emotional *dependence* on a person, which was never God's design. This creates in the spiritual realm an ungodly soul-tie. It is ungodly because it is outside of God's design and plan. It causes a person's identity to become overly intertwined with and dependent on someone else in a toxic way. In fact, it's as if that other person has taken on the role of God in one's life. (This is not to say that we can't have healthy relationships and connections with others. They just need to be in their rightful place: secondary to our relationship with God.)

How do we know if we have depended too heavily on another person to help us feel secure and loved or to validate us? Well, have you ever said anything like the following:

- "I don't know what I would have done without her/him."
- "I don't think I would have survived if she/he hadn't been there for me."
- "She/He rescued me."
- "She/He is (was) everything to me."
- "I don't know what I would do if I lost her/him."

We must have the proper and godly perception of Who is the *most* important person in our life. As a Christian, that person should always be God. God is our Rescuer. God is our Sustainer. He is our Deliverer. In Him is everything we need. Had that person (mother, father, sibling, spouse, friend, whoever) NOT been in your life or not been as awesome as he or she was, GOD would have provided love and care for you some other way—whether it was through another person or directly to you through your relationship with Him.[8] Our confession should therefore be:

- "I don't know what I would have done without *God* providing such an amazing mother/father/spouse/sibling for me. He/she wasn't perfect, but he/she was amazing."
- "I don't think I would have survived had *God* not been there for me and made my mom/dad/spouse/sibling who she/he was."
- "*God* rescued me through her/him." Or "God used her/him to rescue me."
- "He/She is amazing, but *God* is everything to me."

The first set of confessions above put someone else on a pedestal, elevating them to a place they don't belong. The latter confessions conversely and rightly give *God* all the glory and put Him in His proper place... on the throne of our heart. Don't think this is just semantics. It's not. It's a heart attitude and a righteous perception that gives all the glory to God.

A soul-tie can be formed with just about anyone or any*thing* if we become *dependent* on that person or *thing* for love, comfort, and security. I'm not talking about an infant being dependent on its parents. This is normal. But take note, the infant gradually grows up and out of that dependence. This is the healthy progression of life. The problem comes when a child doesn't grow up and out of that dependence on mom/dad for love and safety, or as they grow, they begin to look for other people and things to attach to and draw love from, creating toxic relationships of dependence.

I once heard a story of a child who became *overly attached* to the kittens that the family's cat bore. When it came time for the kittens to go to their new homes, the child had an absolute emotional melt down each time one left. Her mother realized what had happened and prayed to break the soul-tie her daughter had developed with the kittens. The success of her prayer became evident very soon after when the next kitten left their home. This time, the child had very little emotional response, in fact, didn't even notice as she continued to play in her bedroom. The young girl had apparently been cured of her temper tantrums and melt downs around the kittens she had grown attached to.

Every ungodly soul-tie is an opportunity for the devil to oppress us. It is also an opportunity for demons that may be attached to the souls of others to also attach to us for the purpose of oppressing us, making us sick, or just plain making our lives miserable. It is therefore imperative that we break ungodly soul-ties through repentance and prayer.

The term "soul-tie" is not in the Bible but at the very core, the issue is idolatry. Who or what do you trust in? Who or what do you *think* you actually *need*? And who or what are you *relying* on? If the answer is not "the Lord," you likely have an idolatrous dependency that the devil is taking advantage of.

Jeremiah 17:5-10, in the New Living translation says this:

> This is what the LORD says: "Cursed are those who put their trust in mere humans, who rely on human strength and turn their hearts away from the LORD.

> They are like stunted shrubs in the desert, with no hope for the future. They will live in the barren wilderness, in an uninhabited salty land. "But blessed are those who trust in the LORD and have made the LORD their hope and confidence. They are like trees planted along a riverbank, with roots that reach deep into the water. Such trees are not bothered by the heat or worried by long months of drought. Their leaves stay green, and they never stop producing fruit. "The human heart is the most deceitful of all things, and desperately wicked. Who really knows how bad it is? But I, the LORD, search all hearts and examine secret motives. I give all people their due rewards, according to what their actions deserve." (NLT)

Psalm 118:5-6 & 8-9 says:

> In my distress I prayed to the LORD, and the LORD answered me and set me free. The LORD is for me, so I will have no fear. What can mere people do to me?... It is better to take refuge in the LORD than to trust in people. It is better to take refuge in the LORD than to trust in princes. (NLT)

Psalms 146:3-9 says:

> Do not put your trust in princes, *nor* in a son of man, in whom *there is* no help. His spirit departs, he returns to his earth; in that very day his plans parish. Happy *is he* who *has* the God of Jacob for his help, whose hope *is* in the LORD his God, Who made heaven and earth, the sea, and all that *is* in them; Who keeps truth forever, Who executes justice for the oppressed, Who gives food to the hungry. The LORD gives freedom to the prisoners. The LORD opens *the eyes of* the blind; The LORD

> raises those who are bowed down; The LORD loves the righteous. The LORD watches over the strangers; He relieves the fatherless and widow; But the way of the wicked He turns upside down.

As mentioned, the main way a soul-tie is formed is through sexual intercourse. This is why God's design was for us to have sex in the confines of marriage—and *only* in the confines of marriage. When we have sex outside of this boundary, we end up becoming one flesh with people who aren't our spouse, and because we are in sin, the soul-tie is automatically ungodly. The connections with previous partners hang on and cause all sorts of problems in our lives—especially in our marriage. Soul-ties can be to blame for intrusive sexual thoughts, temptation to watch pornography, sexual dreams, and many other related sexual problems. So, let's take care of them. Let's repent and break ungodly soul-ties.

PRAYER TO BREAK SOUL-TIES WITH SEXUAL PARTNERS

> "Lord, I confess that I have not kept Your commands or followed Your ways in regard to sex. I confess, God, that I have had sexual relations with others outside of marriage. I confess that through my fornication I have placed my partner(s), the need for their love and affection, and my fleshly desires above and before You in my heart. I have replaced You as my first love, broken my covenant with You and formed ungodly covenants with others. I am sorry, God, and I repent. I ask for Your forgiveness. Thank You, Lord, that when I confess my sins to You, You are faithful to forgive me and cleanse me from all unrighteousness. Thank You for Your forgiveness.

I choose to forgive myself and receive Your forgiveness in its fullness. I now break and renounce all ungodly soul-ties, unions, influences, and covenants, in body, soul, and spirit that I have formed with [identify partners by name]. I release [say each name again] back to You, God, and I ask You to heal the wounds in her/him/them that caused her/him/them to seek out our union, and I ask You, God, to cause her/him/them to become all You created her/him/them to be. I pray that she/he/they would come to know You and experience Your love.

I also ask, Lord, that every part of myself that has been tied to the others would be washed in Your blood and brought back to me. I call back to myself every piece of my heart that I gave away in sin, and I ask You, Lord, to heal every wound in me that made me seek out an ungodly union. Heal me and make me whole in You. Thank You, God.

In Jesus' name, I now break every ungodly union and transference from their bloodline to mine and every curse empowered through our sin I now cut off from my blood, my life, my soul, my body, my marriage [if applicable], my family/children [if applicable], my destiny, and my future. I break and dis-empower every evil force sent to carry these curses out. In Jesus' name, I bind and renounce every unclean spirit, every spirit of lust and perversion, every spirit of rebellion, disobedience, witchcraft, infirmity, sickness, and disease that has gained access to my life. Thank You that You hear my prayer and love me unconditionally. All glory and praise be Yours, Amen."

Next, we will tackle probably the most difficult and emotional part of this book: recovery from sexual abuse, sexual molestation, rape, and any type of sexual activity that you did NOT consent to.

Hold tight, friend, to the hand of Jesus. He is with us. He has promised to never leave us or forsake us, and He loves us with an everlasting, perfect love. If you're confused by that, it's okay. We will talk about the conundrum in your heart about why He seemingly didn't intervene and prevent the abuse that happened to you. It's a very normal reaction to what you've been through. There is no shame in your questions. Okay, so when you're ready, let's go together. I am not completely ignorant to this experience.

---

[8] Psalm 68:5-6, "A father to the fatherless, a defender of widows, is God in his holy dwelling. God sets the lonely in families, he leads out the prisoners with singing;" (NIV).

6

THE PIT OF PITS

The Lord is close to the brokenhearted and saves those who are crushed in spirit. The righteous person may have many troubles, but the Lord delivers him from them all…
(Psalms 34:18-19 NIV)

When we seek the Lord and submit to Him, He will orchestrate and work miraculous things in order to heal and deliver us. However, some readers may need help navigating through this chapter and the associated prayers. I am not a professional; I am simply a woman who has been counselled by the Holy Spirit and led through her own bondage by Him, who has learned a lot through experience, study, and prayer. Please use wisdom and be self-aware enough to know when you need more support. Depending on how much trauma you have suffered, you may need professional help and a *plan* for healing through an extended period of time. Modalities like EMDR may be helpful but I would highly recommend that you seek a Christian professional who counsels from a biblical perspective and uses healing prayer in his/her practice. Having said that, there will be many who will be set free simply by sincerely working through what is offered here with the Lord. Please continue reading in private, without distractions, when you have a good chunk of time to process and pray.

How does one begin to talk about something as heinous as sexual abuse and/or molestation in its many forms? It has looked different for every victim, and the spectrum of perpetrators is wide. The perpetrator could have been anyone—young, old, family member, friend, the brother of a friend, a babysitter, the older boy down the street, neighbor, father, brother, sister, uncle, cousin, boyfriend, colleague, priest, churchgoer, and even a pastor. The perversion and lust that leads someone to commit the crime can affect anyone at any age.

Statistics tell us that one in three women have experienced sexual violence/abuse at some point in her life—with millions affected in *childhood*. Childhood…

.

.

.

Before the age of twelve.

.

.

.

Many younger.

.

.

It's very difficult to think about. However, we must run to Jesus and be healed. We cannot stay in the pit of pits, either haunted by our experience or falsely indifferent with toxic emotions buried, making us sick. We cannot live at peace nor fulfill our godly assignments on the earth if we are not set free.

My experience happened when I was eighteen, at a party, where I was drinking heavily. My boyfriend and I stayed overnight at his friend's house, and I barely remember going to bed before I passed out. Even though I was unconscious, it was clear in the morning that a lot had gone on and that I had lost my virginity. It actually took me several years to realize that what had happened to me was date-rape. I had not consented to intercourse; I wasn't even conscious. And I wonder to this day if he drugged me and whether he was the only one who violated me.

But praise God! He is my Just Defender and my Healer. He takes what the enemy meant for harm and turns it around for good. He takes my mess and makes it a message. And He restores my soul like it was never broken.

Some time in the spring of 1999, I sat in the passenger side of the car on the long ride home from Toronto… thinking… and watching the trees and farmland go by. Being alone with one's thoughts *can* be an unpredictable place but this particular time, my thoughts were focused, for the most part, on the Lord and His work in my life. I was grateful that the Lord Jesus reached down when I was 22 years of age and rescued me as He revealed the full truth of Who He was and is. This led me to think of my younger years as well as the young man and the painful event he perpetrated; it had caused anger and hate to live in my heart for a long time and that hate and anger didn't glorify God. It didn't serve me or Him. So, in that car on that long drive, Pappa God gently began to dig it out.

It's funny where our thoughts can wander on long car rides, but I suddenly began to think that perhaps one day I would write a book. What a weird thought to think when writing books was never ever something I considered. It was akin to thinking one day I would fly to the moon! *Now*, it doesn't seem outrageous, but back then, I had NO idea I would be here now. And I had no idea that my thoughts were prophetic in nature.

My thoughts continued to wind down the Holy Spirit highway. Over twenty-five years ago, with no idea at all that I would be an author, I thought...

Maybe I will write a book about my experience...

And perhaps my perpetrator will find it and read it...

Then, maybe as he reads, he will realize that what he's reading is actually about him...

That he is the perpetrator mentioned...

That what he did years ago was actually date-rape...

Maybe then he will be sorry, be convicted...

Repent, and give his life to Jesus...

Maybe then he would become a Christian.

At that moment, with all these thoughts coming all unpredictable and such, going in this direction and that... my last thought, *maybe then, he would become a Christian*, stopped me in my tracks. It caused me to sit in utter freeze mode for several moments.

My thoughts continued...

Wait...

If he becomes a Christian, that means he WILL be forgiven for his sin…

And that means…

He will be forgiven for what he did to me…

And that means…

(insert a big sigh and a huge knot in my stomach)

I will need to forgive him too…

If God forgives him, I need to forgive him...

…

Lord, have mercy.

This was weighty. And if you've been through something similar, you know what I mean.

I really did not feel that I could do it *nor* did I want to, initially. The Holy Spirit really needed to help me with this one.

Of course, I know now that as disciples of Christ, we are required to forgive those who hurt us, even when they, the perpetrators, are not believers themselves, but back then, this was the thinking process I needed, to realize that the Lord wanted me to forgive him *and* that I *needed* to forgive him for my *own* benefit. I've got to admit; it took me a minute. It took me a HOT minute… or two… or ten… to want to forgive and get through it.

It's not where we want to go, is it? When someone takes advantage of us in that way? No. We want them to be held responsible and pay the consequences of their actions. We want them to somehow feel the hurt they caused us. We don't want them to just get off the hook. But that is where I needed to go in that moment. Thank God that He's patient with us! In conclusion, the Lord gave me what I needed to follow His will and when we got home that day, I felt so much lighter and free.

That was the beginning of my healing. There were more stages of healing and forgiveness to come but it was a great start. God was coming through for me as my great Healer and my faithful Deliverer.

Psalms 34 reminds us that the Lord delivers us out of ALL our troubles—even the ones that seem too awful to be true—the ones that are unbearable, agonizing and tormenting. Here's part of Psalms 34 in the New Living Translation:

> I prayed to the LORD, and he answered me. He freed me from all my fears. Those who look to him for help will be radiant with joy; no shadow of shame will darken their faces. In my desperation I prayed, and the LORD listened; he saved me from all my troubles. For the angel of the LORD is a guard; he surrounds and defends all who fear him. (Psalms 34:4-7 NLT)
>
> The LORD hears his people when they call to him for help. He rescues them from all their troubles. The LORD is close to the brokenhearted; he rescues those whose spirits are crushed. The righteous person faces many troubles, but the LORD comes to the rescue each time. (Psalms 34:17-19 NLT)

A Psalm from my childhood always brings me comfort. Here is Psalms 23 with my own commentary added:

> 1 *"The LORD is my shepherd,"* the One Who watches over me, guides me, and protects me. *"I shall not want."* I have everything I need.

2 *"He makes me lie down in green pastures;"* He causes me to rest amid abundance. *"He leads me beside the still waters."* He knows how to bring me peace.

3 *"He restores my soul; He leads me in the paths of righteousness for His name's sake."* He heals me and even when life gives me the sourest of lemons, He teaches me and empowers me to be righteous and holy, laying down all my anger, hurt, and pain.

4 *"Yea, though I walk through the valley of the shadow of death, I will fear no evil."* When I've been through the worst, I will not fear, for He is with me and will heal me. *"For You are with me; Your rod and Your staff, they comfort me."*

5 *"You prepare a table before me in the presence of my enemies; You anoint my head with oil; My cup runs over."* While my enemies are still around me, and adversity is on every side, You, God, intervene and serve me, placing a feast of succulent food before me—looking after my every need. Even when life's challenges are still present, You, God, bless me abundantly. Let my enemies see Your favor on my life and be reminded that they are defeated.

6 *"Surely goodness and mercy shall follow me all the days of my life; And I will dwell in the house of the* L*ORD* *forever."* There will never be a time when I am without You, God. You, God, are my dwelling place where I am safe and secure.

Selah.

Leaning on the Everlasting God, finding refuge in His arms is our only healing and saving option.

So, what's your story my friend? How old were you? How long did it go on? Was it one time? Or many? Who did you tell? Anyone? Did they believe you? Did they do anything about it?

What emotions have been flooding your heart?

Confusion?

Anger?

Betrayal?

Fear?

Hate?

Shame?

Between 1 and 10, what's your pain level?

…

…

…

I'm sorry.

…

…

So very sorry.

Just holding space for you, dear one.

…

…

We can't rush through this.

…

…

You deserve to grieve.

…

I can't physically sit with you and hear your story, but God can. In fact, He wants you to tell Him your story…

from your perspective… with all the gritty details and all the emotions…

how it made you feel.

Your heart needs to be validated.

And Jesus is waiting to do that for you.

I invite you now to talk to God out loud—to put words and a voice to your experience. Let go of all the religious rules you've been taught about how we're supposed to converse with the Almighty and instead talk to Him like He's your best friend. Talk to Him like He's sitting across the table from you, or lying beside you in your bed… wherever you are… He's right there with you.

Any shame that would try and prevent you from speaking out loud and telling God about it MUST be denied. We must not cooperate with shame again! Any thought that God is going to be disappointed or disgusted or whatever with you, is a lie. It is from the pit of hell. Remember my dream? The dream where Father God showed up at the worst possible time? There was no shame in His eyes. No shame in His invitation to come to Him. No shame. Only love. He has the same love and acceptance for you despite what you've been through.

Holy Spirit, come and give your daughter courage in this moment!

He is for you always! He loves you, at all times, in every circumstance. And He will never forsake you.

Trust Him.

PRAYER

"Jesus, I have something I need to tell You. You know it already but You're my best friend and I know You want us to tell You everything... to not try and keep secrets from You. So...

When I was... years old... someone took advantage of me... They ... and they ... It was traumatizing. I remember feeling frozen ... and not being able to escape. I was so scared and confused. It made me feel ...

[After telling Him your story and your feelings] Lord, I give You the trauma I felt in those moments. I give You the fear. I give You the confusion. I give You the sense of betrayal. I give You the ... [name all the feelings you felt].

[Imagine putting all your trauma and feelings in a bowl and giving that bowl to Jesus. Name all your feelings separately as you put them in the bowl. Imagine Jesus in your mind's eye. Give Jesus the bowl. Watch Him take it and watch what He does with it. Realize that He is communicating with you through your imagination in picture form. What you're seeing is actually happening in the Spirit realm.]

Thank You, Jesus. [Continue to converse with Jesus as He leads you.] *Thank You, that I can trust You. Thank You that You hear me and believe me.*

I know it is tempting to just rush through and say the prayer so you can say that you said it, but it won't do any good. For a prayer to be effective, we *must* bring our heart into agreement with it (we cannot just say it without meaning it) and we need to pray in faith, believing that what we are praying is being heard and received by the Lord and also accomplished in the Spirit realm.

If you hear a voice in your head that says, *I don't know why I'm doing this; it never works*, this is a demon of unbelief speaking to you. Turn away from it and renounce it. Pray the following: *"Lord, I repent for unbelief. I turn from it now, in Jesus' name. Please forgive me. I renounce unbelief and I command unbelief to be silent now, in Jesus' name."* If it continues, you may need to fast and continue to pray to shut it down. The Lord may show you a root that needs to be pulled up, like a moment in time when you did not believe the Lord.

There is going to be multiple steps for our healing in this one chapter. Telling God your story and your feelings is step one. And if you've done that, way to go. It takes courage to put voice and words to everything that happened. When you do that, you bring it out of hiding and into the light.

OFFENDED WITH GOD

If you've *not* been able to tell God your story yet, let me ask you, "Why?" Are you wondering why God would have allowed the abuse to happen? Are you experiencing anger at God and asking, "Why didn't He protect me?" If so, those are valid questions. Let's talk about it.

Many precious sisters are trying to make sense of their suffering but can't. They don't understand why God seemingly did not intervene in their circumstances. You wonder, *why did God not stop it?* My friend, I believe, if He could have stopped it, He would have. But God cannot *control* the actions of a person who has free-will and is likely under the influence of demons. He can, however, heal you of your wounds and restore you. He can and will heal your heart, if you will repent for blaming Him and being angry at Him.

Several years ago, the reality of how many people blame God for the adversity in their lives gripped me and a prophetic word bubbled up. It fits with our discussion, so here it is:

> "The Lord would say to you, "Don't give in to deception. Don't believe the lies of the enemy. Beware, he prowls around like a roaring lion seeking whom he may devour. Don't be devoured by his lies. Have I [God] not said, "I am for your good, not for your destruction?" Have I not said, "I am for you?" Have I not said, "You are mine and I am yours?" Have I not given My all to rescue your soul and have I not said, "It is finished?" Have I not waited and longed to be known by you just as I know you? And I say to you, "Know Me! *Know* Me. Know *Me*."
>
> My heart is gripped this morning with a message I must convey. I have seen it repeatedly and the same issue comes up continually before me as I minister to others. It sits in front of me like a flashing neon sign that can't be ignored. It must be exposed.
>
> I see beloved ones covered in ashes, the remains of a life and heart once lived but no more. I see beloved ones suffering and trudging through their days with nothing but grief, their lives destroyed by another. Lives crushed in the grip of a vicious spiral of sin, hurt, anger, blame, offence, bitterness, unforgiveness, and hate. It ends in death, but where does it begin? Know this. Know where it begins, and you can avoid it altogether. Misunderstanding God. Not knowing God and blaming God. "Well, He is sovereign, right? He is

in control of everything, right? If He wanted to, He could stop that person in my life from hurting me, from sinning against me and knocking the wind right out of me, right? But He doesn't. He just sits by and watches." Yes, or no? This is the question that demands an answer. Have you had this dialogue in your head? Is this what you believe? If it is, you my friend are deceived. This is where it begins. It begins with a distorted belief about Who God is and Who He is not. It begins with believing the lies the enemy is feeding your mind about God's stamp of approval on your hurtful circumstances.

Here's the truth: You have an enemy and his name is Satan and Satan's number one goal is to drive a wedge between you and God—to cause you to become offended at Him. As soon as Satan gets you to agree with that, you are in big trouble. You are out of bounds, out of fellowship and you are free game for the devil. Don't do it! Know your God!

Herein lies the tension: sovereignty verses free-will. Contrary to popular persuasion from the enemy, sovereignty and free-will are not contradictory. They exist simultaneously, and both are true. God is sovereign. He is God and there is no other. He is the One Who made you and the universe and put all the laws in place. He is the One Who created order out of chaos. He is the One Who decided on the rhythm of life and decided that living things would reproduce after their own. He is the One Who breathed His breath of life into you. He is also the One Who decided at the beginning of time to place man over the earth—to appoint us to steward the earth and rule over it and He is the One Who is eternal and just and doesn't, in fact, can't, go back on his Word, even when we mess up. He is the One Who despite His power and authority, chose to give *us* authority on His earth and chose to work through man. He is the One Who sovereignly chose to limit Himself by giving us free-will—free choice to serve Him or not serve Him, free choice to love or not to love.

God did not want puppets or robots that He could control. He wanted family—a people who *chose* to love Him. He wants relationship with us—authentic relationship with a true heart connection. Does God attempt to intervene? Yes! Does God attempt to sway our heart toward the right choice? Yes! Does He move by His Spirit and put love beyond our own ability in our heart? Yes, of course He does. He can because He's God but ultimately, we do have the final choice. By His sovereign will He gives us extra grace and the ability to say "no" to sinful things [1 Corinthians 10: 13]. He does not allow us to be tempted beyond what we can bear, and He provides a way out for us, but we must choose that way out. We must resist the devil and choose what is right. Unfortunately, some of us fail at that. Sometimes the people in our life choose the wrong way, even after God has done all He can to try and stop them, and they end up sinning against us still. Sometimes the people in our life hurt us beyond imagination and God's heart grieves. He sees and His heart aches. He sees our tears, our broken heart and broken life and He weeps for us. My friend, stop shaking your fist at God. It is only providing the devil with more ground to encroach upon. It is only serving to defeat you further. Realize that none of it is God's fault. Resist being offended at God and praise Him for Who He is. Thank Him for being faithful to you in all seasons. Know that God is good and His mercies for you are new every morning. Know that God's heart for you is for the restoration of all things and that He is walking with you, even carrying you through it all, to the other side.

If you will do this and continue, despite what has happened to you, forgiving all who have hurt you, then, you will see restoration of joy, peace, hope and love and you will be victorious in Christ. God is your answer and your Defender, not your enemy. You are extravagantly loved by the Creator of all. This is the truth that we must bind ourselves to even amid pain and trying circumstances, even amid evil coming against us in its fullest form. Stand with God in truth. Submit to His Lordship, stay rooted and firmly planted in the truth of God's Word and resist the devil. Resist his evil manipulations of your mind, resist being offended, resist hate and he must flee. Simply put, God is love. If what has happened to you is not love, it wasn't God and He did NOT approve of it. God is love and God is good... all the time."

I hope this has helped you to understand things a bit better. Now, let's pray to come out of agreement with anger toward God.

PRAYER

"Father God, I repent for being angry at You and blaming You for the abuse I suffered. I realize now that it was not Your fault and that You did not

> want it to happen. I am so sorry for misunderstanding You, God. Please forgive me. Thank You, God, for Your forgiveness. I receive it now in its fullness. Help me now to trust You again and share my heart with You completely. Fill me with Your Spirit and Your empowering grace. In Jesus' name, amen."

Now, go back and begin the previous prayer again, sharing your story with God including all the details and feelings you felt. If you felt abandoned by God at the time, tell Him about it. Tell Him all of it. Don't try to protect anyone and don't try to hold it together. Allow yourself to feel the full weight of it all, trusting the Holy Spirit to keep you through it.

LUST OR LOVE

At this time, I'd like to expose something that won't apply to everyone but will indeed be vital for someone's freedom. I am not an expert, but I believe, when sexual abuse happens repeatedly in childhood, especially when the perpetrator is someone who is supposed to love us, such as a parent or grandparent, there is deep, overwhelming confusion. It is possible that a child who was abused by a parent or grandparent learned to wrongly interpret sexual behavior as love and they struggle to accept that what happened was inappropriate. To further complicate things, our flesh in general is wired for pleasure and doesn't differentiate between right and wrong; it just knows what it enjoys. So, a young child who has had a sense of physical pleasure from the abuse can be completely devastated by shame as an adult or can struggle to see or admit that the behavior was abuse. If that is you, please understand that God knows and He understands it all. He created us! And He knows how we are wired.

Let me pray for you:

Right now, in the authority of the Lord Jesus Christ, I come against every lie wanting to hold you captive and I bind it and break its power now, in the name of Jesus Christ of Nazareth! I stand on behalf of my sister in Christ now, and I intervene on her behalf and I say, "No more lies! No more shame!" You are worthy of love. You are worthy of perfect and holy love from God—the right kind of love that upholds you, honors you, and protects you.

I say the Spirit of Truth is now infiltrating your heart and mind, leading you to Himself, drawing you in and delivering you from all unclean spirits causing confusion. I command all confusion to go now, in Jesus' name.

I renounce the lie (on your behalf) that a family member's love sometimes includes touching private parts. I renounce the lie that this is okay. I renounce the lie that some family members only know how to love that way so we should let them. No! That's a lie! I renounce the lie that daddy wanted a "special" relationship with you so that makes it okay. I renounce the lie that some daddies express love differently than others, including touching private parts. I renounce the lie that if you keep it a secret, it's okay. We come out of agreement with these lies now, in the power of Jesus' name. And I break them off you now! I break the power of deception in your mind now, in Jesus' name. Deception, go! Break! Break! You are not welcome here. Your time is up! Truth, come! Truth come and enlighten your mind now, in Jesus' name.

The fog is lifting. The shroud that has kept you in confusion is lifting now. I remove the shroud from your mind, and I say clarity of mind is coming upon you now, in Jesus' name. I bind your mind to the mind of Christ. I say you shall know the truth and the truth is making you free. Right now.

I come against the self-hate, self-rejection, and self-harm that has come on the heels of the shame and I break them now, in Jesus' name. It is not your fault! It is not your fault! I cancel and break the blame off of you now, in Jesus' name. You are not to blame. You were an innocent child with no understanding of right and wrong and no ability to overcome an adult who you trusted to treat you right. You were manipulated in your mind to submit to the authority of an adult who did not have your best interests at heart. That adult's mind was twisted and distorted by the enemy. It is not your fault. Release the false guilt now, in Jesus' name. Put the false guilt down at the foot of the cross. Put the shame down. Put the self-hate, the self-rejection and the self-harm down now, in Jesus' mighty name; they don't belong to you. They are not yours.

...

Sit in that for a minute friend. Let the Holy Spirit minister.

...

...

Let yourself grieve. Let yourself just grieve for a minute.

...

The truth is... some of you were groomed. Some of you were set up to accept the bad behavior well in advance of it happening. I'm sorry. I'm so sorry you have gone through that.

Please take some time with the Lord and let Him love you.

Go to YouTube and search up the songs:

- *Heal Me* by Faith Worship Music
- *Healing in His Wounds* by GPA Worship (Ali McFarlane)

- *The Hem of His Garment* (Intimate Worship Song) by Upper Room
- *All Men are Broken* by Misty Edwards

Sit with the Lord and let Him minister to you through these songs. When you're done, come back and continue through the following prayer.

PRAYER

> Pray only what applies to you: "Lord God, I repent for believing lies about how I was treated. I repent for not wanting to believe it was abuse and that it was wrong. I repent for making excuses for my family member and how they treated me. *[If applicable]* I repent for wanting it to be okay. Please forgive me. I come out of agreement with the shame attached to this and I completely reject shame, in Jesus' name. It does not belong to me. I decide right now, Jesus, that I am going to accept your mercy and grace over my life, and I will not accept the lies of the enemy connected to my worth. Lord, heal the wounds of my heart. I need you desperately. Holy Spirit, come and meet me where I'm at. Thank You, God. In Jesus' name, amen."

Pray and repent for self-hate, self-rejection and self-harm:

> "Lord, God, I repent for accepting the false guilt of what happened to me. I repent for believing it was my fault. I repent for hating myself and my gender *[if applicable]*. I repent for rejecting myself and my gender *[if applicable]*. And I repent for harming myself, for cutting myself, and for burning myself, in Jesus' name *[if applicable]*.

> I ask You, God, to forgive me of all these things. I know that You created me just as I am and I know that You did not create junk. In fact, You created me with beauty in mind. I choose to forgive myself for hating myself and my gender, rejecting myself and my gender, and for harming myself, and I receive Your forgiveness God in its fullness. Heal the wounds of my heart, God. In Jesus' name, amen."

ANGER

Can I be completely honest with you? Nothing makes me angrier than child sexual abuse. It grieves my heart so. I'm sure it has made you angry too.

However, is simply being angry a sin? That's a good question.

Let's look at Jesus for a moment. Was He ever angry? Yes. Mark 3:1-5 says the following:

> And He (Jesus) entered the synagogue again, and a man was there who had a withered hand. So they watched Him closely, whether He would heal him on the Sabbath, so that they might accuse Him. And He said to the man who had the withered hand, 'Step forward.' then He said to them, 'Is it lawful on the Sabbath to do good or to do evil, to save life or to kill?' But they kept silent. And when He had looked around at them *with anger*, being grieved by the hardness of their hearts, He said to the man, "Stretch out your hand." And he stretched it out, and his hand was restored as whole as the other. (brackets and italics added)

Notice in this passage that Jesus' anger was connected to the grief in his heart, "being grieved by the hardness of their hearts." This is holy righteous anger. His heart was grieved because the Pharisees had no compassion in their heart for this man with the withered hand. Having compassion on others and doing something about it when it is within your power, is godly. But the Pharisees were more concerned about following the rules than a fellowman's wellbeing. Jesus was rightfully angry; His anger was motivated by injustice.

Did Jesus sin when He was angry? No. The Bible tells us that Jesus was without sin. I John 3:4-5 says, "Whoever commits sin also commits lawlessness, and sin is lawlessness. And you know that He was manifested to take away our sins, and in Him there is no sin." Hebrews 4:15 says the following, "For we do not have a High Priest who cannot sympathize with our weaknesses, but was in all points tempted as we are, yet without sin." Jesus was without sin. So, the righteous anger He felt could not have been sin.

In summary, being righteously angry is not sin. *We, as humans,* do however need to be careful about being angry for selfish reasons, for instance, being angry because we didn't get our way. This is a whole different scenario. The motivation for the anger in this case is sin which could, in my opinion, make the anger sin as well, but you can seek the Lord on that one for yourself later. That's not really what we're talking about in this book.

Although *righteous* anger in and of itself is not sin, when we are *righteously* or *rightfully* angry, we *can fall* into sin depending on what we do with it and how we act because of it. Now I assumed for a long time that "don't sin in your anger" meant don't *tear a strip off* someone because of your anger. Don't explode on someone; don't "blow your top." I think I thought that way because I experienced a lot of that as a child. Yelling and emotional abuse was common in my childhood home. But let's look at Ephesians 4:26 to learn more. It says the following:

> "And 'don't sin by letting anger control you.' Don't let the sun go down while you are still angry, for anger gives a foothold to the devil" (NLT).

Whoa! Anger gives the devil a foothold. Yikes. But not because you're angry... because you've held onto it too long and because you've allowed it to control you. In other words, don't let anger be the motivation for your actions. Don't act out of anger. And don't seek revenge.

In order to not sin in our anger, let's come out from under the oppression and pressure anger can put on us by admitting our anger to God... every... single... day. "Do not let the sun go down while you are still angry," means don't sleep on it. Talk to God about it.

Also notice, I'm NOT saying, "Admit and process your anger by talking about it with a friend" so you can simply *unload* your feelings. No. It's not about simply unloading our feelings, though that can be helpful when done with the right person, in the right spirit, for the purpose of healing. But simply wanting to unload on someone is not godly; it's gossip and it's offense looking for a place to be heard.

Simply wanting to unload our feelings on someone is gossip and offence looking for expression and a place to land.

Unloading our feelings on someone can get us entangled with demons of gossip and offence, especially when we do it repeatedly. No, we need to talk to God about our anger because He's the One with the answers; He's the One with the right Words to help us. So, w*ith God*, resolve your anger every day; tell Him about it and allow Him to speak to your heart, diffuse your fuse, give you understanding and compassion to open your heart again, to bring you back to a place of peace. A friend does not have the power to do that. Only God does. First and foremost, tell God about your anger and why you are angry, with all the details. For our purposes right now, hopefully you've already done that in the previous step. We just simply need to add this confession to our prayer:

PRAYER

"God, I'm angry. What happened to me was unjust. And I'm mad; I've been mad for a very long time. Father, forgive me for holding onto my anger for so long. I repent. I should have come to You sooner with it. Help me God. Please pour out Your mercy and Your grace. Give me understanding. Give me wisdom. Give me compassion again. I'm angry at … because… Why would he/she do that to me? (Now, sit and listen to how God responds. Take notes if you want so you can remember what He says or shows you.)

Thank You, God, for your help and power in my life. In Jesus' name, amen."

Good job.

As we continue on in this healing journey, we must consider whether we told someone about the abuse and what they did about it, if anything. There are two issues here that can be open doors for the enemy. First, if you didn't tell anyone about the abuse, your silence translates in the demonic realm as agreement and consent; in this case, we must repent for not telling someone so they could intervene. Of course, fear would have played a huge role in your silence, so you should include that in your prayer as well. Secondly, if the person you did tell didn't believe you or did nothing to stop it, forgiving that person is a must.

PRAYER

Pray the prayer that fits your situation:

"Heavenly Father, I repent for not telling someone about the abuse. I repent for listening to the fear of not being believed or the fear of getting into trouble or being punished. Please forgive me. I should have told someone what was happening. I didn't want it to continue but felt frozen by fear. I didn't know who to trust. Thank You, God, for forgiving me. I renounce my agreement with the fear, and I renounce my agreement with the abuse now, in Jesus' name. I break the covenant I unintentionally made with perversion, abuse, and victimization through my silence. In Jesus' name, amen."

"Heavenly Father, I repent for holding onto anger at … (person's name) for not believing me when I told her/him about the abuse. I repent for holding onto anger at … (person's name) for not stopping the abuse when I told her/him about it, for not protecting me, and for not seeming to care about how I was being hurt. Please forgive me, God. I should have released this anger to You a long time ago. I repent for the bitterness in my heart toward her/him. And I repent for the unforgiveness that has been in my heart all this time toward her/him. Please forgive me. I choose to forgive (person's name) for not intervening and protecting me as she/he should have. I release her/him. And I receive Your forgiveness and cleansing for myself, God, in its fullness. In Jesus' name, amen."

The next step in this process is uprooting hate and forgiving our perpetrator(s). We have processed a lot so far, but there is more to go. Now we will allow the Holy Spirit to take a deep dive in our heart to remove any hate we feel and give us the grace we need to forgive.

HATE AND FORGIVENESS

"But I don't want to forgive!" I know. I didn't either. But we actually don't have a choice, friend.

Matthew 10:8 shares with us a vital principle in the Christian faith: *"Freely you have received, freely give."* And Matthew 6:15 says, *"But if you do not forgive men their trespasses, neither will your Father forgive your trespasses."* If we want Father, God, to forgive us, we must forgive others, regardless of how awful the offense. The good news is that it is normal for us as humans to not have what it takes. You're not alone in that. We need to seek the Lord to give us what we need and most of the time, it is a powerful reminder of our own salvation, healing, cleansing and deliverance that propels us forward into the ability to forgive others.

We cry out to the Lord, *"Help me want to do this! Not my will God, but Yours!"* Our will can hold us back. Our will is selfish by nature. However, after we are born-again, we can choose to crucify our own fallen will and submit to the will of the Father. But it is by choice! It doesn't happen automatically without your consent. So, pray, *"I choose right now to submit to the will of the Father, in Jesus' name. Give me Your heart, O God."*

Admitting to God the hate you feel in your heart is also a choice. But sometimes we need the power of the Holy Spirit to break the deception that keeps the hate buried and undetected. Let me tell you about my experience with hate.

In the spring of 1990, my husband and I took a lovely vacation to Western Canada. We stayed at the amazing Chateau Lake Louise, visited Banff, Alberta, and took many scenic hikes through the mountains. We decided to begin to try to start a family with this once-in-a-lifetime trip. I expected to be expecting very soon after, but my expectations were dashed when over a year later, I still was not pregnant.

I had experienced much trauma as a young girl regarding pregnancy—watching my mother go through two painful miscarriages, receiving evil reports from my mom about her doctor, way too much information for my age and experiencing maternal neglect due to my mother's mental illness. All these emotionally traumatic events left bleeding, open wounds in my soul that were affecting me as I tried to conceive.

After some prayer counseling, I conceived for the first time but quickly found myself in tears, grieving a miscarriage at 8 weeks gestation. I held the phone to my ear as I solemnly explained to my parents that I had miscarried. Dad's words of compassion were comforting but mom's comments were far from it. "Well, you weren't really pregnant anyway." Jaw dropped, breath... stopped. I don't remember my response. All I remember is the blade cutting my heart, creating yet another wound. In hindsight, I know that my mom's reaction was just her way of coping. My miscarriage must have triggered her horribly as in her forties she suffered at least two herself with no healthy emotional healing.

After hanging up the phone, I sat with my prayer counselor friend, venting to her about all the ways my mother had hurt me. Under the unction of the Holy Spirit, she calmly but very directly asked me, "Do you hate your mother?" Her question shook me to the core. I wanted to blurt out, "No!"

but couldn't. While the Holy Spirit held my tongue, it felt like time stood still. Conviction overtook me as the Lord pulled back the curtain of my heart. I was mortified by what was there. Hot tears streamed down my face as I whispered my confession, "Yeah, I guess I do." *What kind of person was I?* I thought. The answer of course was, "A person with wounds of the soul who had been purchased by Jesus and invited to be renewed by grace," but for a moment I felt the shame of my sin. It was not my finest moment, but the Holy Spirit did His work. The Lord forgave me, I forgave myself, and I forgave my mom for many things.

As it turned out, forgiving my mom and releasing the hate that was in my heart, was the final doorway to my healing of childlessness. [For my full story, see my book *Barren no More: Prayer Strategy for Every Believer Experiencing Fertility Challenges.*] My husband and I went on to having four beautiful children, including a set of twins, one girl and three boys in total. It's amazing how the will of God is unlocked in our lives when we choose to fully align with Him and His will—when we are willing to submit our whole heart to Him.

Is it possible that hate, which has been sitting in your heart possibly undetected, has held you captive? Is it possible that it has kept you from being able to spiritually grow and develop into your spiritual gifts and God's plan and purpose for your life?

> Behold, You desire truth in the inward parts, and in the hidden *part* You will make me to know wisdom. Purge me with hyssop, and I shall be clean; wash me, and I shall be whiter than snow. (Psalms 51:6-7)
>
> Create in me a clean heart, O God, and renew a steadfast spirit within me. Do not cast me away

> from Your presence, and do not take Your Holy Spirit from me. Restore to me the joy of Your salvation, and uphold me *by Your* generous Spirit. *Then* I will teach transgressors Your ways, and sinners shall be converted to You. (Psalms 51:10-13)
>
> Search me, O God, and know my heart; try me, and know my anxieties; and see if *there is any* wicked way in me, and lead me in the way everlasting. (Psalms 139:23-24)

This is the cry of my heart. "Make us pure, O God!" I pray it is also the cry of your heart.

We are called to love our enemies. It's not easy, but yet, that is the requirement. Hate the world but not people. Hate the sin but not people. Hate what they do, but not the people themselves. Hate the demons that are behind their actions but not the people. Jesus died for the people. Jesus loved them enough to die for them too.

God help us! Let's pray.

PRAYER

> "Father God, search my heart. Reveal to me any hate buried there. *(wait on God)*
>
> *Confess:* "Lord, I confess that I hate ... *(say the person's name).* I am sorry. I understand that You died for them and that You have died for all people regardless of their actions—regardless of how hurtful their behavior. You even died for Saul who became Paul in the New Testament. Saul grotesquely murdered Christians yet You called him and saved him, then sent him out to evangelize the world. Your ways are not our ways. Help me,

God. Give me understanding. Give me wisdom. Give me grace and mercy. Give me compassion and a heart that is willing to yield to what I don't understand in my own mind. I choose to submit to You and Your ways. I completely turn away from hating … *(say the person's name)*. I renounce hate, Lord, and I ask You to forgive me. I choose to forgive myself for having hate in my heart and I receive Your forgiveness, God, in its fullness.

I also choose to forgive … *(say their name)* for … *(say what they did to you)*. I choose to forgive him/her. I choose to let go of the right to get back at him/her and the right to be offended. I completely let him/her and it go so I can be free and unhindered in my walk with You, God. Thank You, Jesus, for the grace to pray this, to agree with it, and to walk this out. These are not just empty words but the confession of my true heart.

I now break and renounce the soul-tie with *(the person you hated)* which was formed because of my hate. I release *(their name)* back to You, God, and I ask You to heal the wounds in him/her that caused him/her to operate in gross sin, and I ask You, God, to cause him/her to become all You created him/her to be. I pray that he/she would come to know You and experience Your love. I also ask, Lord, that every part of myself that has been tied to him/her would be washed in Your blood and brought back to me. I call back to myself every piece of my heart taken from me, and I ask You, Lord, to heal every wound in me created by hate and victimization. Heal me and make me whole in You. Thank You, God. In Jesus' name, I now break every ungodly union and transference from their bloodline to mine and every curse empowered through this sin, I now break and cut off from my blood, my life, my soul, my body, my marriage *(if applicable)*, my family/children *(if applicable)*, my destiny, and my future. Thank You, Jesus, for what you've done for me. Thank You for Your mercy and grace. Holy Spirit, come and fill me afresh. In Jesus' name, amen."

Forgiveness is a choice. We do not wait until we "feel" like forgiving. If we did, we'd be waiting our whole lives. No. We make a choice despite what we feel, and we confess with our mouth, *"I choose to forgive."* Then each time the enemy reminds us of the offense, and we are tempted to take it up again, we confess out loud the following:

"No, I choose to forgive him/her. I choose to let it go. I will not ruminate on this anymore. I will not rehash the past. Every voice that is not God, I command it to be silent now, in Jesus' name. It is finished. In Jesus' name, amen."

We continue in this manner until we are no longer harassed by spirits that want us to gossip or ruminate on our hurt. We can share our story with one trusted person for the purpose of bringing it into the light and being healed, but that is all. We should no longer need to rehash the past with anyone. You can continue to talk to God about it but not any other person. I do believe that there is even danger in speaking repeatedly to a therapist about it because the devil has a hidden agenda; he wants us to continue to rehash so that we can never be free from it. He wants us to remain offended; each time we tell the story we are offended all over again. Forgive, forgive, and forgive again, then move on. Sometimes it's two steps forward and one back, but whatever you do, continue to forgive and let it go. Do not continue to tell your story repeatedly. Some people will do this to receive sympathy. Don't do it. It will cause you to remain in a victim mentality and identity.

"Come up here!" says the Lord. *"Come up here with Me! The air is cleaner! The atmosphere pleasing. The fellowship sweeter."* Don't settle for fellowship that is twisted, relying on sad stories and sympathy. Instead, fellowship with the Lord, over truth, Who He is on your behalf, and over your healing and freedom.

> It is for freedom that Christ has set us free. Stand firm, then, and do not let yourselves be burdened again by a yoke of slavery. (Galatians 5:1 NIV)

I remember hearing a commercial on the radio for a collision repair shop. Their slogan was, "We repair your car like the accident never happened." The Holy Spirit wants to heal you to the point that it's like the abuse never happened. Friend, you can't get to that place if you keep revisiting the "collision." Let it go. It's in God's hands now. He is your avenger. Romans 12:19 says, "Beloved, do not avenge yourselves, but rather give place to wrath; for it is written, "Vengeance is Mine, I will repay," says the Lord." We will all stand before the judgement seat of Christ and give an account, including us (see 2nd Corinthians 5:10). God is a good and faithful Judge. If something is not covered in the blood of Christ, consequences will be paid some other way. Let it not be us; the wrath of God is no joke. Let us pray that all perpetrators find salvation, forgiveness, healing, and deliverance offered to them through Christ. Let's pray for our enemies. Pray that they will be delivered from the wrath of God, especially those who have caused little children to suffer. Matthew 18:6-9 says the following:

> "Whoever causes one of these little ones who believe in Me to sin, it would be better for him if a

> millstone were hung around his neck, and he were drowned in the depth of the sea. Woe to the world because of offenses! For offenses must come, but woe to that man by whom the offense comes!
>
> "If your hand or foot causes you to sin, cut it off and cast *it* from you. It is better for you to enter into life lame or maimed, rather than having two hands or two feet, to be cast into the everlasting fire. And if your eye causes you to sin, pluck it out and cast *it* from you. It is better for you to enter into life with one eye, rather than having two eyes, to be cast into hell fire.

Sin is serious stuff—serious enough that we should cut body parts off if they cause us to sin. Lord, have mercy.

How else has the sin perpetrated against you caused you to respond or react in sin? Here's a few more possibilities that we will explore in the next chapter: bitterness, judgements, and inner vows.

Hang on friend. We've got a few more steps to our complete healing to process.

7

BITTERNESS, JUDGEMENTS, & INNER VOWS

Pursue peace with all *people*, and holiness, without which no one will see the Lord: looking carefully lest anyone fall short of the grace of God; lest any root of bitterness springing up cause trouble, and by this many become defiled…
(Hebrews 12:14-15)

We see from this verse in the heading, that bitterness is a root that springs up and causes trouble with the potential to defile many. Where does bitterness come from? Bitterness is the result of long-standing anger that has been left to mature and grow in the heart. In fact, synonyms of bitterness are anger and resentment.

What type of defilement can come out of bitterness? Well, I think revenge, hate, and any act that tears a person down either with words or deeds… gossip, slander, suspicion, insults and the like. One such "fruit" of bitterness we absolutely need to address in this book is judgements.

Matthew 7 (NLT) begins in verse one with, "Do not judge others, and you will not be judged," and people living in sin love to pull this verse out of their pocket to manipulate anyone who attempts to confront them about their waywardness. This is why it's really important to have a fully rounded understanding of judgements, so we know how to confront people and when it *is* appropriate and not appropriate. What does a righteous judgement look like and what does a sinful judgement look like? In short, a judgement made out of bitterness is sinful. But let's learn a bit more so we can understand it fully. Matthew 7 goes on to say the following:

> For you will be treated as you treat others. The standard you use in judging is the standard by which you will be judged. "And why worry about a speck in your friend's eye when you have a log in your own? How can you think of saying to your friend, 'Let me help you get rid of that speck in your eye,' when you can't see past the log in your own eye? Hypocrite! First get rid of the log in your own eye; then you will see well enough to deal with the speck in your friend's eye." (Matthew 7:2-5 NLT)

Notice it doesn't say, "Don't help your friend." It says to take care of your own issue first, then help your brother or sister.

I will incorporate some text from my book, *Position Yourself for Healing* to help us further as follows:

A Christian is called to live in the power of the Holy Spirit, a life worthy of the blood of Jesus—a life of consecration. We are called to first cooperate with the Lord in the process of sanctification through responding in repentance to the conviction of the Holy Spirit as He identifies the planks and the splinters in our own eyes. Only then, after we have been filled with the Spirit and submitted every area of our life to the Lord, will we ever be called to come alongside a brother or a sister *in love* to remove a speck from their eye. Only then are we prepared to encourage and exhort others for the purpose of restoring, building, and calling others to a higher place in Christ. Please note, I am not suggesting we must be perfect... instead fully submitted. Galatians 6:1 encourages us to do this:

> Brothers, if anyone is caught in any sin, you who are spiritual [that is, you who are responsive to the guidance of the Spirit] are to restore such a person in a spirit of gentleness [not with a sense of superiority or self-righteousness], keeping a watchful eye on yourself, so that you are not tempted as well. (AMP)

Notice the phrase, "in a spirit of gentleness [not with a sense of superiority or self-righteousness]." This is key!

Matthew 18:15-17 gives us further instruction if the person we have come along side, in humility, refuses to listen to us. We are told by Jesus Himself to go as far as exposing their sin to church leaders:

> "If your brother or sister sins, go and point out their fault, just between the two of you. If they listen to you, you have won them over. But if they will not listen, take one or two others along, so that 'every matter may be established by the testimony of two or three witnesses.' If they still refuse to listen, tell it to the church; and if they refuse to listen even to the church, treat them as you would a pagan or a tax collector. (Matthew 18:15-17 NIV)

This is serious stuff! Those in the church *who are followers of Christ*, are not supposed to still be entangled in a *pattern* of sin. And if it's obvious that they are, they need to be encouraged *in gentleness* to repent.

Some versions of Matthew 18:15-17 specifically speak about those who sin *against us*, however, some versions like the NIV quoted above, do not. I would say that if a brother or sister in Christ is part of our church family and they are involved in a *pattern* of *blatant* sin, they *are* sinning against us; they are pretending to be something they are not. Their sin affects the whole church family whether it is done in private or against us in particular. Having said that, I think it's also important to mention here, the following: the local church isn't the same now as it was in the New Testament (at least in North America). Most churches in North America *do not* follow the New Testament blueprint. In the NT, the apostles went out into the community, preached in the streets, and brought *converts* into their church gatherings. They did not invite pre-believers into their meetings. Their gatherings were private.

In the popular North American church with open doors, some purposefully made palatable to pre-believers, not everyone who attends has surrendered their lives to Christ; not everyone in the church has been regenerated by the Holy Spirit nor have they been empowered to live free of sin. Today, believe it or not, some people only come to church for its social benefits. So, greater discernment is needed! Let's be sure that if we're confronting someone in kindness regarding something we see in their lives, that they have *indeed* made a decision for Christ, been born-again and possess the empowerment of the Spirit. We can't expect someone who still lives in darkness to behave like they're in the light.

It's always good to have sisters (and brothers) in the Lord who are willing to be sharpened and who will sharpen us in a loving and respectful relationship. What's not good is when someone leaves a conversation feeling less than, shamed, unheard, unloved, and even humiliated by an exchange. If this happens, it's *possible* that we have not communicated well and *possibly* have operated in a spirit of haughtiness or self-righteousness. However, realize too that there could be situations where a person doesn't want to be sharpened and would rather stay in their sin. This person may be defensive and come away offended regardless of how much compassion and love you attempt to communicate.

The point here is that there are times we are called to judge *righteously* or perhaps better said, *spiritually discern*, when a brother or sister needs help. Other scriptures that support this are 1 Corinthians 2:14-16:

> But the natural man does not receive the things of the Spirit of God, for they are foolishness to him; nor can he know *them*, because they are spiritually discerned. *But he who is spiritual judges all things*, yet he himself is rightly judged by no one. For "who has known the mind of the LORD that he may instruct Him?" But we have the mind of Christ.

As well as 1 Corinthians 5:11-13:

> But now I am writing to you that you must not associate with anyone who *claims to be a brother or sister* but is sexually immoral or greedy, an idolater or slanderer, a drunkard or swindler. Do not even eat with such people. What business is it of mine to judge those outside the church? *Are you not to judge those inside?* God will judge those outside. "Expel the wicked person from among you." (NIV, emphasis added)

We are absolutely to discern and make righteous judgements about the behaviors, attitudes and opinions *of our brothers and sisters without looking down on them* for the purpose of praying for them, as well as knowing how much time we want to spend with them or if we want them speaking into our lives. Sometimes it's our place to address things that we see and sometimes it's not. Sometimes we are called simply to pray for them.

A brother or sister *who has been trained by righteousness* may be *called* by God to lead those they are close to and even the Body of Christ at large, through exhortation; this may include calling believers back to the fear of the Lord and to holiness. To some it can sound critical or like they are judging others, but they are not; they are fulfilling their mandate from God. Think Jonah and Elijah, John the Baptist, and the Apostles.

I wonder how the people felt initially when Peter stood up among them in Acts 2 and boldly confronted them about their sin? Peter stated to them plainly when talking about Jesus, "...you, with the help of wicked men, put him to death by nailing him to the cross" (Acts 2:23b NIV) and called them to repent. Was Peter being judgmental? Was he being critical? No. He was preaching the truth boldly and doing what he was called to do. Peter was called to confront people in their sin so they would turn away from it. Three thousand people were added to the church in one day because of Peter's bold confrontation.

In John 7:24, Jesus addressed a crowd in the temple court where He had been teaching, regarding judgments made against Him for healing on the Sabbath. Jesus says to them, "Do not judge by appearance [superficially and arrogantly], but judge fairly and righteously" (John 7:24 AMP). Jesus had come into the temple teaching something different—something fresh—and moving in a way that seemed wrong on the outside (healing on the Sabbath) because it challenged the way they had always done things (according to the law), so they had to make a judgment. Was what they were hearing and seeing, God, or was it not? They had to decide whether they were going to believe what He taught.

We are faced with the same thing every day. We see *Christian* memes on Facebook, and we need to make a judgment whether it lines up with our belief system—the Word of God. We listen to a preacher online and we must qualify everything they say with the Word and decide, are they biblical in their teaching and are they led by the Spirit? Is it beneficial to listen to this person? Will it build me up in my faith or lead me into deception?

Other questions to consider are, "Do they have pure motives?" "Do they have integrity?" and "Can they be trusted?" The answers to these questions we can't possibly know by outside appearance because many people are very good actors. They say all the right things. They are funny, charming, knowledgeable, and likeable. Yet, some are influenced by demons of pride, people pleasing, flattery, greed, and/or lying. The only way we will know is by asking the Holy Spirit to lead us and show us the truth of who a person is. *This* is making a *righteous judgement*—by and with the wisdom of God through the Holy Spirit. *However*, making a righteous judgement still does not include forming a *negative* opinion of someone from a place of hate, offense, or bitterness.

Let's look at more scriptures in the Bible that tell us *not* to judge.

Let's consider Romans 2:1. Romans 2:1 begins with the word, "Therefore," and anytime we see *that* word, we should look back in the scriptures to establish context. Let's begin with Romans 1:28-32 which is talking about those who have chosen to reject God. Here's the New International Reader's Version for simplification:

> They didn't think it was important to know God. So God let them continue to have evil thoughts. They did things they shouldn't do. They are full of every kind of sin, evil and ungodliness. They want more than they need. They commit murder. They want what belongs to other people. They fight and cheat. They hate others. They say mean things about other people. They tell lies about them. They hate God. They are rude and proud. They brag. They think of new ways to do evil. They don't obey their parents. They do not understand. They can't be trusted. They are not loving and kind. They know that God's commands are right. They know that those who do evil things should die. But they continue to do those very things. They also approve of others who do them. (NIRV)

Romans 2:1 now follows:

> Therefore you have no excuse *or* justification, everyone of you who [hypocritically] judges *and* condemns others; for in passing judgment on another person, you condemn yourself, because you who judge [from a position of arrogance or self-righteousness] are *habitually* practicing the very same things [which you denounce]. (AMP, emphasis added)

It's obvious from Romans that those who are in gross sin certainly have no business judging anyone. However, those who are spiritual and led by the Spirit also need to be extra careful what they think about people and what they do with what they see in the natural and in the Spirit (or what they discern by the Spirit).

Google's dictionary defines the verb, *to judge* as: "to form an *opinion* or *conclusion* about."[9] The word "conclusion" indicates something that is *final*, which means *we've made up our mind*.

We naturally form opinions and draw conclusions about words, messages, and behaviors all the time and this is good. We need to discern what is godly and what is not, without becoming offended. What we're not supposed to do is draw *definitive negative conclusions* about *people*, their character and their identity; this is the danger zone.

I may see or observe that a person is not behaving in a godly way, but the *only opinion* or *conclusion* I should come to is that *they're struggling*, or *they need Jesus (or more of Jesus)*, and I should pray for them. *Never should I decide that they must be a bad person without hope or redemption—without the capacity to grow or change.* We do not know anyone's heart outside of the revelation of the Holy Spirit and we are all in a process of sanctification. Just as we see that another person is not perfect, we are also not perfect.

There may be times when we may wonder, *has that person really experienced new birth by the Spirit?* Maybe we haven't seen the fruit of repentance or transformation in their lives. But let's pray for them and give them grace—just as we would want to receive grace from others.

So, when is judging a problem? We can very easily make judgements against people either out loud in words or quietly in our heart, that are rooted in bitterness and anger. What we don't realize is the bitter judgements we've made that define a person's character or identity as something negative cause us to become like that person or cause us to experience the same misfortune they have. It is a spiritual principle. We become what we judge when we judge from bitterness.

In my late twenties, I personally had to work through anger, hate, and unforgiveness toward my mother, which I have already alluded to. She had mental health issues which caused her to be very self-focused and emotionally fragile. She did not look after me well, and I had hate in my heart toward her. Because of this, I had made *bitter judgements* against her. I had *decided* that she was emotionally weak; she could be heard crying in her bedroom behind closed doors often. I could not depend on her for much and I felt to some degree, abandoned by her. Additionally, the fear my mom lived in was obvious. She and my dad tried to instill faith in us from a young age, but my mom seemed unable to live it out herself. Because of all these things, as a teenager and young adult, I looked down on her and *concluded* that she was not a good mother.

In God's perfect time, the Holy Spirit led me to repent for holding judgements *against* my mom and helped me to see her heart from His perspective—from a heart of love, compassion and understanding. Had I not repented, I could have given the enemy a legal right to afflict me in the same way my mom was afflicted with physical illnesses. But in God's kindness, He alerted me to the condition of my heart so I could be whole and in divine health. I love the goodness of God and His faithfulness to correct us when we need it.

I'd like to share another story from my own life here if that's ok. I listed back on page 42 several things that could be fueling our dysfunction. One of them was "*sexually charged, embarrassing* situations that have caused shame and perhaps bitter judgements against others" and I also said that I had a prime example from my own life. It not only is important to bring to God the big, horrific, and super traumatizing things but it is also important not to trivialize anything that could have caused us to make a bitter judgement against someone.

I was in grade eight. I was a very shy, insecure young person and didn't talk to boys much. In our classroom, our desks were organized by twos, so my desk was butt up against another one. We all had a close neighbor and for some of us shy ones, it was a little too close. My *partner* happened to be a boy. Behind us were two girls that were more popular than I. One day, my partner was casually conversing with the girls behind us, and I was kind of on the sidelines when he drew attention to the fact that his fly was not zipped. He was "flying low" as we called it at the time. Instead of zipping his fly discreetly, he made a big deal out of it, and I just naturally looked at what he was doing. He quipped loudly, "Well, don't look!" causing me immense embarrassment. The girls laughed and I was horrified. Because of my embarrassment, I concluded in my heart that he was a jerk... an idiot... a pervert... and a few other colorful names. I did not like him for embarrassing me like that. He did something similar in high school too; he spoke inappropriately about his sexual preferences to the two girls next to him. Uhg! I just kind of rolled my eyes and turned around to face the front of the room, trying to ignore him. But I had to repent for making bitter judgements against his character and identity.

What *conclusive statements, names or judgements* have you spoken or held in your heart about the identity of others because of embarrassment, anger, hate, or bitterness? Have you made *decisions* that define anyone's character negatively which in turn have caused you to look down on them in your heart? Perhaps you've witnessed them being unfaithful or disloyal. Perhaps you've heard them exaggerate or tell half-truths. Or perhaps they've not protected you or defended you as they should have. Perhaps you've been hurt by them, repeatedly. If you've looked down on anyone because of their sin and/or weaknesses and held bitter judgements against them, I invite you now to dig deep—to invite the Holy Spirit to help you and have a conversation with God.

I know. "They deserve it!" If someone has traumatized you, this may be what you feel right now. I get it. If someone acts out against us and sexually abuses us, isn't it obvious that they are a pervert! Isn't it obvious that they are *jerks* and *idiots* and every other derogatory name under the sun? Yes, it's okay to admit your feelings. We need to be completely transparent if we want to get free. Get your frustration out.

This is our flesh and the way of the world, *labeling* people according to their actions, good or bad. I'm not suggesting we can't call out someone's bad behavior and put boundaries in place. I'm saying we can't put labels on people's identity and call people names. Labels stick. Especially when they are spoken out loud. Everyone has the potential to repent and change and become a child of God; let's not lock them in a prison with a label. As a disciple of Christ, we are called to a higher standard. We are *in* the world, but we're not supposed to be *of* the world; in other words, we are not supposed to behave like the world and if we have truly been transformed by the love of Christ, we won't want to. Let the Holy Spirit help you friend.

What about your relationship with your husband? Have your bitterness and judgements against others (perhaps those who have abused you) carried over into your marriage? Perhaps you have not been keen on sex because of your past, and your husband has not reacted kindly. Perhaps he hasn't had much grace for your wounds or hasn't had the emotional maturity to understand you. Or perhaps you have simply carried judgements over and pinned them on your husband too. Perhaps "all men are the same" in your mind. Friend, it's time to repent and be healed. It's time to forgive your husband specifically and repent for being bitter and holding judgements against his character. Don't let pride keep you in this prison.

I invite you to repent now so you can be released from the bondage of bitter judgements. Doing so will bring immense freedom to your mind, heart and possibly even your body.

If you're willing, I invite you to pray something like this:

PRAYER

> "Lord, I confess to You now that I have been bitter toward *[name the person and include your husband if appropriate]* and I have made bitter judgements against him/her/them. I have thought him/her to be *[state your opinions and the labels]* and I repent. I ask You, Lord, to forgive me for looking down on them and thinking less of them than You. I'm sorry. God give me Your heart and perspective of who they are. Help me to see them through Your eyes. I understand that they are not their sin, but they are a person who needs You. Thank You for Your forgiveness, Lord. I choose to forgive myself and receive Your forgiveness fully. Thank You for Your blood, Jesus, that cleanses us and makes us whole. Lord, heal every wound in me that has caused me to have a negative opinion of them. I renounce the judgement that *[say their name]* is a *[say the judgement or label]*. I renounce every negative opinion and/or word I have spoken against him/her/them now, in Jesus' name and I command every negative word and label to fall to the ground, unfruitful. Thank You, Lord. In Jesus' mighty name, amen."

INNER VOWS

Moving on. The three things in this chapter exist in a chain. Bitterness can lead to bitter judgements, and bitter judgements can then lead to inner vows. One perpetuates the other. Inner vows are made to try and control our lives and avoid pain. A vow is simply a promise made to oneself with deep conviction to *never* or *always* do or be something. It is an attempt to protect ourselves from being hurt, either because we've been hurt already, or we've witnessed others being hurt.

When my husband and I were trying to start a family and couldn't, I realized that I had made three vows regarding having children and they were holding me hostage. Firstly, because of trauma in childhood with my mom as I've previously mentioned and accumulating ridiculous amounts of fear around doctors and hospitals, I made a vow when I was an adolescent to *never* have children. Secondly, shortly after moving into our first home after getting married, I didn't like our neighbors (they had parties until all hours of the night, their young son wandered the street late at night unsupervised, and he threw rocks at our dog; I had some valid reasons lol), so I made a vow not to have children while living in that neighborhood. Thirdly, I made a vow not to have children while driving the car we drove as it was very unreliable; it had left us stranded on the highway a few times and I certainly didn't want to have a baby on board in that situation. I was not successful at conceiving and birthing our first-born until all three of these vows were either met or broken in prayer.

I became pregnant for the first time immediately after renouncing my vow never to have kids. Unfortunately, I miscarried. But became pregnant again with our first-born, Jessica, *four* months after moving into a new house and *one* month after buying a *new-to-us* car. All three vows were sin because they were all an attempt to control, but in addition, the first vow was made because of fear, the second was made because of judgements against our neighbors and the third was made because I knew it wasn't wisdom to drive an unreliable car with an infant. Instead of making that third vow, we should have just listened to wisdom and bought the newer car when we needed it.

Once we make commitments to ourselves, we step out of God's plan and into our own. We decide God is not trustworthy and we take things into our own hands. When we do this, we lock the Holy Spirit out of those aspects of our lives and because of our obstinate independence, end up giving the devil an opportunity instead. Guess what? The devil doesn't waste an opportunity.

In my situation, the devil was preventing me from conceiving, and he also caused me to miscarry, but the devil can also cause sickness and mental torment because of vows. I would encourage you to ask the Holy Spirit to remind you of any time you may have stubbornly and emphatically said, "I'm *never* going to [blankety blank]!"

Abuse and the resulting anger, hate, and bitterness can cause us to decide to *never* be like certain people, perhaps our parents, or to *never* treat our own children the same way we were treated. If we were abused, this sounds reasonable as it's obvious not to want to repeat the same sin, however, every vow *to self* always comes from a prideful, independent spirit that does not trust God and puts hope in our own (flawed!) abilities. We should want to trust God! He's the One with the power! We need to trust God. We are only dust. Let's not forget that. John 15:5 says, "I am the vine, you are the branches. He who abides in Me, and I in him, bears much fruit; for without Me you can do nothing." We need help!

In his book, *Shadow Boxing*, Dr. Henry Malone gives a real-life example of someone who was held hostage by her inner vow and bitter judgement against her father, as follows:

> "A grandmother once came to me seeking help. With tears in her eyes, she confessed that she was abused as a child and that she abused her three children. She was troubled by watching her adult children physically abuse her grandchildren. Often, she found herself abusing them, too. "I can't take it any longer. You must help me," she begged.
>
> I asked her to share about her childhood abuse. She was the third of six children. Whenever one child did something wrong, her father punished all six of them."[10]

Dr. Malone goes on to describe the horrific abuse the children suffered but I will spare you the details. He continues as follows:

> "When she was ten years old, she made an inner vow. She promised herself that "if I ever have any children, I will never do to them what Daddy does to us." While she didn't punish them in the exact same way, she beat her children with whatever was at hand... Quickly I saw that the vow she had made had imprisoned her and set her on a track that she could not get off simply because she had judged her father. When she repented of her inner vow and asked God to forgive her for judging her father, freedom came. We broke the vow and its results ceased."[11]

Bitter judgements and inner vows can keep us locked into behaviors we don't want to be a part of! We need to get free.

Let's look at a Bible passage that clearly says we are not to make vows or take oaths because we do not have the power to keep them.

In Matthew 5:33-37 Jesus says the following:

> "Again you have heard that it was said to those of old, 'You shall not swear [take an oath] falsely, but shall perform your oaths to the Lord.' [you will be bound to them] But I say to you, do not swear at all: neither by heaven, for it is God's throne; nor by the earth, for it is His footstool; nor by Jerusalem, for it is the city of the great King. Nor shall you swear by your head, because you cannot make one hair white or black. But let your 'Yes' be 'Yes,' and your 'No,' 'No.' For whatever is more than these is from the evil one. [brackets mine]

So, what is *more* than a simple 'Yes' or 'No'? A 'Never' is more. An 'Always' is more. Do not think that you have the power in and of yourself to say, "I will *never* do that." Or "I will *always* be this." And your flesh may want to continue to argue against what I'm saying here. So, I am going to continue to explain this, and I declare that all arguments and all self-justification will cease, in Jesus' name.

It is impossible for us to fulfil a promise to ourselves in our own strength. We need God in everything we do. We can say, "What my parents did was wrong, and I forgive them, but I don't want to do what they did, so I will need God's help and power to be better," instead of, "I will *never* be like them." Do you see the difference? One is humble and one is bitter, prideful and self-righteous. The *vow* assumes that you are so much better than them.

Recognizing the promises/vows we've made to ourselves in pride and *in our own power*, repenting, asking the Lord for forgiveness, and breaking our promises and vows to self will lead us into freedom and we can do that now. Pray something like this:

PRAYER

"Lord, I confess that in judgement, pride and an independent spirit, I have tried to control my own life in my own strength by making a vow. Father God, I repent for wanting to be in control of everything, for pushing You out of my life, for not trusting You and not relying on You, Your power and Your authority. I repent for thinking that I was self-sufficient without You. I repent for relying on my own strength instead of You. Lord, I ask for Your forgiveness. I renounce the vow that I will never/always *[repeat the vow]*. I cancel those words in Jesus' name, and I now break my agreement with them. I command them to fall to the ground, fruitless. Father, I bring every part of myself and my life back under Your authority, care, and protection and I choose to trust You with my life. I ask You again, God, to be Lord over EVERY part of my life. I choose to forgive myself for making this vow and I now break and cut off every curse that has come from my disobedience and desire for control. I break the power of every evil force that was released to carry out these curses over me, my family, my destiny, and my future. I thank You, Lord, that my family and I are covered in the blood of Your Son, Jesus, and that He has redeemed us from every curse by becoming a curse for us. Thank You, Lord, that when we confess our sin to You,

> You are faithful and just to forgive and cleanse us from all unrighteousness. I receive Your forgiveness and cleansing, and I give You praise. Fill me afresh, Lord, with Your Holy Spirit to overflowing and baptize me again in Your power. In Jesus' most powerful name, Amen."

One last application of this topic...

I sense the Holy Spirit very strongly showing me to address the following: some readers, of course not all, when they were little, played "wedding" with their daddy where they pretended to get married. Perhaps you played this out in actuality or perhaps you imagined it very intensely or had a very vivid dream about it. We need to address the "vows" you may have said while playing out the "pretend" wedding. If this scenario happened with anyone else, like an uncle or anyone else who was an adult, please replace "my father" with the name of the person in the prayers below. (I am *not* talking about marrying someone in a Satanic ritual; this you need to see a Christian trauma-informed counsellor/therapist about as well as a deliverance minister. Do not attempt to address that kind of demonic ritual without help.)

We also need to re-visit soul-ties as in the previous situations, whether it was the "pretend" wedding or sexual contact, a soul-tie would have been formed. So, we will deal with the vow taken in a "pretend" wedding and soul-ties in the next prayer.

PRAYER

Confess what is applicable and replace "my father" with the name of the individual with whom you took the vows:

- "Father, God, I confess that my father and I pretended to get married and took vows with one another. I thought it was just fun, but I know now that I should not have spoken vows to my father nor should he (she/they) have spoken vows to me. I repent. Please forgive me."

- "Father, God, I confess that I actively participated in an imaginative wedding with my father and he (she/they) and I spoke vows to one another in my imagination. I repent. Please forgive me for using my imagination for ungodly purposes and forgive me for taking vows with my father in my heart."
- "Father, God, I bring to You a very vivid dream I had where my father and I got married and took vows with one another. I ask You, God, to intervene and break every agreement and covenant erroneously made in the dream and I cancel my participation with it. I break the power of our words and command them to fall to the ground, in Jesus' name."

Continue:

"I renounce the vows that we took and spoke. *[Be specific if you can: "I renounce the vow that I will always…]*

I choose to forgive my father for his (her/their) participation and for leading me in ungodliness, in Jesus' mighty name. I also choose to forgive myself. I didn't know any better. Thank You, God, for forgiving me; I receive it.

I now break and renounce all ungodly soul-ties, unions, influences, and covenants, in body, soul, and spirit that were formed with my father *[or any person you spoke vows with in a mock or pretend marriage ceremony].*

I also break and renounce all soul-ties, unions, influences, and covenants, in body, soul, and spirit formed through the sexual abuse I experienced from *[name every person who sexually molested or abused you].*

I release *[say each persons' name]* back to You, God, and I ask You to heal the wounds in him (her/them) that caused him (her/them) to operate in this sin.

I ask, Lord, that every part of myself that has been tied to him (her/them) would be washed in Your blood and brought back to me. I call back to myself every piece of my heart that was taken from me, and I ask You, Lord, to heal every wound in me created by fear, abuse, and victimization. Heal me and make me whole in You. Thank You, God.

In Jesus' name, I now break every ungodly union and transference from their bloodline to mine. Every curse empowered through the sin of taking vows, sexual abuse and sexual molestation, I break and cut off from my blood, my life, my soul, my body, my marriage *(if applicable)*, my family and children *(if applicable)*, my destiny, and my future. Holy Spirit, fill me to overflowing. Saturate me, God, in Your mercy and grace. Thank You for hearing my prayer and seeing my heart. In Jesus' name, amen."

We will cover complete deliverance from dark spirits in the last part of the book. It's important that we cover all our bases with confession, repentance, and renunciation first.

---

[9] Google dictionary

[10] Dr. Henry Malone, *Shadow Boxing* (Lewisville: Vision Life Publications, 1999), 78. Print.

[11] Malone, *Shadow Boxing*, 78. Print.

8

LIES WE BELIEVE

For You formed my inward parts; You covered me in my mother's womb. I will praise You, for I am fearfully *and* wonderfully made; Marvelous are Your works, And *that* my soul knows very well. (Psalms 139:13-14)

Back in chapter 2, Who's Who, we talked about who we are in Christ. However, any type of abuse that we have suffered can cause us to believe lies about our identity. This in turn makes it difficult for us to receive God's love and grab hold of the truth of who we have become in Christ. The truth is: we have become brand-new creations. The old is gone and the new has come. We are re-born in Spirit, and we have become part of God's family with a new bloodline. We have a new inheritance. Hallelujah.

Let's ask ourselves, though, do we really believe it? And do we live from that place? Maybe we have the head-knowledge but not the heart-knowledge or the revelation of it for ourselves. What does it take for this truth to penetrate our heart, our soul—mind, will, and emotions? For us to believe it for ourselves—not just for others, but for us? What is preventing us from believing it, for real, deep down inside?

I submit to you that there is a group of lies the enemy convinces us of that in turn perpetuate continued circumstances in our life to support them. The main lie is this: "I am not loveable." Perhaps even, "I am not likeable." From there we have a bunch of other lies that hold us in a prison of worthlessness, helplessness, hopelessness, and powerlessness. All lies! We are none of those things... BUT strangely enough the circumstances in our life many times will confirm these lies to us. "Well, my father didn't want me." "I was rejected over and over by others." "I was abused and treated badly." We think that all these circumstances provide the evidence of our rejection and worthlessness. But God does NOT say that over us. So, here's my challenge: Who are you going to believe? The devil? The broken messed-up world we live in? The circumstances orchestrated by the devil? Or God?

The choice is yours.

Whoa! "It's that easy?" Yes.

It's that easy.

We can decide who we are going to listen to and believe. We can decide for ourselves whose word we are going to put value in.

We live in a broken, fallen world and the devil is constantly working to undermine us and tear us down. In fact, the devil had a plan right from the beginning (for many people, from the womb) to break our heart and to make us believe we are worthless and unlovable. You see, if he can get you to agree with those lies, he has basically stripped you of your ability to have impact in the world. Why? Because if you lose your confidence, you won't step-out. You won't be bold. And you won't be courageous. You will sit in lies. In fear. In rejection. Not doing or saying anything that influences others for their good, including the gospel. The devil ends up shutting your mouth and stealing your voice. If you are going to fulfill your assignments from God on the earth, you need to have a voice (or impact, whether that's through your vocal cords, writing, braille, sign language, or acts of service/benevolence).

All people have intrinsic value simply because they were created by God in His image. Your value does not diminish because of Adam and Eve's fall. Your value does not diminish because of your sin or the sin of others that has wounded you. ALL of us need forgiveness and salvation because of sin but...

Our worth in God's eyes is confirmed by the very act that secured our redemption... the ultimate sacrifice of His Son.

God the Father and Jesus would not have carried out their extraordinary and painful plan if we were not worth it to them.

"But why would someone reject me or abuse me? Doesn't that mean I'm worthless?" No! People reject us because they either don't see our worth or they don't like what we offer, which usually is the light we carry. Darkness in others is very often the reason; darkness does not like the light! People abuse us because of the darkness lurking inside them—the darkness that hasn't yet been expelled by the light of God.

Remember what Jesus said in John 15:18-21 as follows:

> "If the world hates you, remember that it hated me first. The world would love you as one of its own if you belonged to it, but you are no longer part of the world. I chose you to come out of the world, so it

> hates you. Do you remember what I told you? 'A slave is not greater than the master.' Since they persecuted me, naturally they will persecute you. And if they had listened to me, they would listen to you. They will do all this to you because of me, for they have rejected the one who sent me. (NLT)

People reject you because of Jesus in you. They abused you because their heart had not yet been transformed by the love of Christ. Even if they went to church, it does not mean they were surrendered or even saved, let alone transformed. There are people who are "Christians" by name only and there are *true disciples of Jesus*. There is a big difference! And then there are Christians who still struggle with perverse desires, who need deliverance. The abuse we suffer is *never* about a lack of worth in us.

Let's identify the lies we believe. How do we do that? First, we need to ask the Holy Spirit to search our heart—to pull the curtain back and reveal to us the deep things we don't even realize are there. We need to allow the Holy Spirit to see it all—the embarrassing things, the messy things, and the private things. And we need to be willing to accept what He shows us. We can't live in denial any longer. We can't live in self-protection anymore. The time has come for us to be completely honest and vulnerable with God and ourselves. PLEASE don't check out at this point or skip over this content because you erroneously believe that there are no lies you believe. Lies are sneaky. Sometimes the lies have just become normal, and we don't even realize they are there. We just continue to function from them as if they're truth.

Some might not want to give up their lies because it's the lies that are keeping them safe. Perhaps you're believing, *I won't survive any other way*. Your beliefs can be coping mechanisms. They can be a way to self-protect. Very often the lies keep us out of relationships and out of the risk of being rejected. People have hurt us, so we conclude that people are unsafe. Some people are unsafe, but not all.

God has given us the discernment we need, in our spirit, to know who to trust and who not to trust. He is with us, warning us, speaking, and directing us. As an adult who is born-again *and* baptized in the Spirit, we have the ability to hear His voice and follow His lead. God is not asking us to trust everyone. He's asking us to trust Him to lead us and He's asking us to be obedient to His ways. (If you are not yet *baptized* in the Spirit, go to Appendix B and come back. To learn more about hearing God's voice, go to Appendix C.)

We have got to find our safety in the arms of Christ. We have got to find our confidence in Him. And trust Him completely.

I'd like you to consider reading and meditating on Psalms 139. This is a Psalm David wrote about himself, but it is also about you as God's creation. So, as you read it, read it slowly and personalize it for yourself. Read it slowly.

> O LORD, you have examined my heart and know everything about me. You know when I sit down or stand up. You know my thoughts even when I'm far away. You see me when I travel and when I rest at home. You know everything I do. You know what I am going to say even before I say it, LORD. You go before me and follow me. You place your hand of blessing on my head. Such knowledge is too wonderful for me, too great for me to understand! I can never escape from your Spirit! I can never get away from your presence! If I go up to heaven, you are there; if I go down to the grave,

> you are there. If I ride the wings of the morning, if I dwell by the farthest oceans, even there your hand will guide me, and your strength will support me. I could ask the darkness to hide me and the light around me to become night—but even in darkness I cannot hide from you. To you the night shines as bright as day. Darkness and light are the same to you. You made all the delicate, inner parts of my body and knit me together in my mother's womb. Thank you for making me so wonderfully complex! Your workmanship is marvelous—how well I know it. You watched me as I was being formed in utter seclusion, as I was woven together in the dark of the womb. You saw me before I was born. Every day of my life was recorded in your book. Every moment was laid out before a single day had passed. How precious are your thoughts about me, O God. They cannot be numbered! I can't even count them; they outnumber the grains of sand! And when I wake up, you are still with me! (Psalms 139:1-18 NLT)

It's so comforting to know that God is so near and that He was the master craftsman knitting us all together from the deepest places of our soul to the outer parts of our body. He actually knows exactly how many hairs are on your head at all times.

> Are not five sparrows sold for two copper coins? And not one of them is forgotten before God. But the very hairs of your head are all numbered. Do not fear therefore; you are of more value than many sparrows. (Luke 12:6-7)

Let's begin to unravel the lies.

For now, bring your heart into agreement and say these things out loud with me:

"In Jesus' name, I renounce the lie that I won't survive if I give up the lies I believe."

"I renounce the lie that I need to protect myself because God won't."

"I renounce the lie that I need to protect myself because no one else will."

"I renounce the lie that I am unlikeable."

"I renounce the lie that I am unlovable."

"I renounce the lie that I am unlovely."

"I renounce the lie that I am helpless."

"I renounce the lie that I am hopeless."

"I renounce the lie that I am a mistake."

"I renounce the lie that I am powerless."

"I renounce the lie that I am worthless."

"I renounce the lie that I don't matter."

"I renounce the lie that I never get it right."

"I renounce the lie that I'm a screwup."

"I renounce the lie that I'm a loser."

(What other names or labels were put on you? If any, renounce the lie of that label.)

"I renounce the lie that I was not wanted." You, my friend, were wanted by God. That is why He created you.

"I renounce the lie that the circumstances of my conception and/or birth determine my worth." Your worth is determined by God and the truth that He created you. You are His masterpiece. (See Ephesians 2:10) You were predestined to be His.

"I renounce the lie that I am a reject."

"I renounce the lie that I am inferior."

"I renounce the lie that I'm not good enough."

"I renounce the lie that no one likes me."

"I renounce the lie that how people treat me determines my worth."

"I renounce the lie that God loves some people more than me."

"I renounce the lie that I am damaged goods."

"I renounce the lie that I am trash."

"I renounce the lie that I will be broken forever."

"I renounce the lie that I am irreparable."

"I renounce the lie that my purity is gone forever."

"I renounce the lie that I lack beauty."

"I renounce the lie that I am stupid."

"I renounce the lie that I'm not worth it—worth the effort, worth the pain, worth getting to know, worth spending time with, worth the inconvenience, worth working through the disagreement..."

PRAYER

> "Father God, I repent for believing lies. I repent for accepting rejection. I repent for putting greater value on peoples' opinions of me than Your opinion. Please forgive me, God. I renounce rejection. I renounce worthlessness. I renounce being unlovable. I renounce unlikableness. I

renounce unloveliness. I renounce helplessness. I renounce hopelessness. I renounce powerlessness. I renounce unworthiness. In Christ, I am lovable, likable, lovely, powerful, helpful, hopeful, worthy, accepted, favored, beautiful, smart, valuable, wonderful, and seen.

I declare that I can stand up for myself in a godly way, in humility and meekness. I declare that my God makes me strong and courageous as I submit to Him. I accept God's forgiveness. And I declare that my God is my Protector and Defender. I am not God, but I am also not a worm. I needed forgiveness and I have received it. I accept my identity as a loved, redeemed, and favored daughter of the King, fearfully and wonderfully made. Thank You, God. In Jesus' name, amen."

Praise the Lord. We are on the right track. Hallelujah. The Lord is healing your perspective and the way you see yourself. Come, Holy Spirit, do what only You can do.

Let's continue by talking about the iniquity that travels through our bloodline.

9

STEWARDSHIP OF OUR FAMILY LINE

Then God blessed them, and God said to them, "Be fruitful and multiply; fill the earth and subdue it; have dominion over the fish of the sea, over the birds of the air, and over every living thing that moves on the earth." (Genesis 1:28)

God's original mandate to us as His creation was to have dominion over the earth and subdue it. Subdue means to:

- conquer or defeat: to gain mastery over, using force if necessary;
- control;
- soften or tone down.[12]

Dominion refers to supreme authority, sovereign power, or the right to govern.[13]

Psalms 115:16 says, "The heaven, even the heavens, are the Lord's; but the earth He has given to the children of men." Originally it was our job to steward the earth in a godly way; unfortunately, Adam and Eve failed to do that and lost their place in the garden of Eden. As a result, man lost his dominion on the earth, and it was given over to the devil.

Man died to God, became cursed and enslaved to sin because Adam and Eve failed to obey God. Eve was deceived by the serpent and Adam stood by just watching it happen, abdicating his authority and responsibility to lead. I'm so grateful God had a plan for us to recover.

In the New Testament, when the devil tempted Jesus in the wilderness, he took Jesus up on a high mountain and showed Him all the kingdoms of the world and their glory and said to Him, "All these things I will give You if You will fall down and worship me" (Matthew 4:9). The devil was empowered to offer this because he owned it all; he was in control (for the time being). The devil tempted Jesus to worship him in exchange for the earth and its glory *without* having to go through the cross, but Jesus denied him. Jesus said, "Away with you, Satan! For it is written, 'You shall worship the Lord your God, and Him only you shall serve" (Matthew 4:10). Of course, the devil didn't know that Jesus and His Father had another plan to get the kingdom and its glory back into our hands but that is exactly what happened when Jesus allowed the sin of the world to fall on Him. In the garden, Satan had won temporarily but was soon overthrown by King Jesus when He rose from the dead. The keys of the kingdom came back to us because Jesus paid our debt in full. Hallelujah! Jesus says the following to Peter in Matthew 16:19:

> "And I will give you the keys of the kingdom of heaven, and whatever you bind on earth will be bound in heaven, and whatever you loose on earth will be loosed in heaven."

In Christ, we have the keys to the kingdom of heaven. Now, we are charged once again with the responsibility to steward well what we have been given.

Stewardship is the "careful and responsible management of something entrusted to one's care. It involves overseeing resources—such as money, property, the environment, our health, body, soul, or our gifts and talents—in a manner that *benefits future generations* rather than serving only immediate personal interests."[14] It involves *"guarding our heart"* and guarding who we listen to in the garden of our mind. Stewarding, managing, and holding ourselves accountable to God through repentance and holy living benefits us and our future generations, but also cutting off what is flowing through our bloodline from *previous* generations which hasn't been previously dealt with also is necessary for our freedom (and health) and that of our descendants. So, let's talk about it.

Do the sins of previous generations affect us? Well, Jesus has paid the penalty for not only our sin but also the iniquity of our forefathers. Our sins are forgiven when we confess and repent. Not before. 1 John 1:8-10 says the following:

> If we say that we have no sin, we deceive ourselves, and the truth is not in us. If we confess our sins, he is faithful and just to forgive us *our* sins and to cleanse us from all unrighteousness. If we say that we have not sinned, we make him a liar, and his word is not in us.

"If" we confess our sins, we are forgiven. Ok, so it works the same way with the *iniquity* that comes from our forefathers. Iniquity is the guilt, weakness, bent of character or perversity that comes down through the generations from deeply rooted patterns of sin which have not been forgiven through repentance. Sin in my life and in yours that we do not repent for and turn away from can become iniquity in our children. Iniquity represents a bent or propensity to sin in a certain way or more plainly said, a corruption of

character that very often manifests into a deep pattern of sin in the family line.

Isaiah 53:5 says the following:

> But He (Jesus) *was* wounded for our transgressions, *He was* bruised for our iniquities; The chastisement for our peace *was* upon Him, And by His stripes we are healed. (brackets added)

This verse mentions "transgressions" and "iniquities" separately because they are two different things. According to blueletterbible.org the original word translated as *transgressions* is *peša*ʿ which can also mean sin, trespass and rebellion.[15] The original word translated as *iniquities* is *ʿāôn* which can also mean perversity, depravity, and guilt.[16]

The best thing we can do is recognize that our ancestors were in sin and ask the Holy Spirit to help us confess their sin and repent on their behalf because we may not have any idea whether they repented or not. Perhaps we know at least in part what our parents were guilty of but what about our grandparents and great-grandparents or even further back? Exodus 20:5 tells us that it can go back to the fourth generation. However, we DON'T need to get all wrapped up in worry and anxiety about it, wondering if we have confessed everything. We simply trust in the Holy Spirit to lead us. He wants us to be free just as much as we do, possibly even more.

Because our focus for this book is lust, sexual dysfunction and perversity, we will focus on those things in our prayers. Honestly, these issues are rarely isolated to one generation. Sexual dysfunction and perversity are usually a pattern through the family, though they are very often kept secret and not talked about.

You may say, "How am I supposed to know what their sexual sins were?" Well, sometimes we know things; sometimes we are given clues, or we have noticed "red flags" in someone's behaviors. If someone is born out of wedlock we know they are guilty of fornication. If they are born before nine months after their parents' wedding, fornication is also likely. If you don't know what to confess, you can pray and ask the Holy Spirit to lead you. And don't allow your carnal mind to talk you out of praying and confessing a certain thing. Something may just pop into your mind, and then perhaps you think, *No! I don't think they ever did that!* Don't talk yourself out of something the Holy Spirit has shown you. He is talking to you through your thoughts. Just confess it. But do NOT allow your heart to go into offense and accusations against someone and don't gossip about it with others. Simply repent on their behalf and let it go.

So, just as back in previous chapters you confessed your own sexual sin based on what the Holy Spirit convicted you of, do the same for your ancestors. If you have trouble hearing the Holy Spirit, consider what you struggle with, what has happened to you and look for patterns with others in your family.

Get a piece of paper and get into the presence of God through worship and prayer. Then pray:

> "Lord, God, what sexual sins are my ancestors guilty of that need to be confessed and repented for?"

Write down everything that comes to your mind whether it's a word or a picture. Perhaps He will lead you to a scripture that will give you clues or remind you of something you witnessed, experienced, or heard in the past.

Just in case you're struggling with this: I bind and break the power of deception and false loyalty over you now, in Jesus' name. I say, "You will be free to hear the Holy Spirit on your ancestor's sin. You will be loyal to God and His purposes over your family." Do not put your family in a high place and please make sure to renounce the lie that honoring your mother and father includes hiding their sin and not holding them accountable. Remember, we aren't broadcasting their sin on Facebook; we are only talking to God about it. There is nothing dishonoring about that. In fact, if you hide someone else's sin by keeping a family secret, you are complicit in that sin and need to repent.

Bring your heart into agreement with the following prayer and speak it out loud sincerely, in faith, believing that what you're praying is effectual:

PRAYER

"Lord, God, I come to you in repentance. I confess to You that my family, my ancestors and I, have not obeyed Your commands; we have not kept Your laws nor honored You with our lives. As a family we have been involved in things that have broken Your heart. We have worshiped other gods—worldly things, sexual desires not of You, our flesh, sexual pleasure, [name other things that your ancestors may have valued higher than God and His ways].

I confess to You, on behalf of my family and ancestors, the sin and iniquity of *[name all iniquity the Holy Spirit revealed to you earlier including things like idolatry, relying on self, narcissism, selfishness, anger, violence, abuse, victimization, hatred, bitterness, unforgiveness, judgements, adultery, fornication, perversion, lust, gluttony, rejection, abandonment, covenant breaking (divorce), incest, and so on].*

I repent on behalf of myself and my ancestors. Lord God, I am sorry, and I ask for Your forgiveness. God, I thank You that You are a merciful God and a God who is patient and long-suffering. I turn from the iniquity of my ancestors now and I receive Your forgiveness in my life and the lives of my family and all future generations. I now choose to forgive my ancestors for their sin, iniquity, and weaknesses and for the negative effects that have come upon my life and the lives of my children. In the name of Jesus, because we are forgiven, I renounce and cut off from my life and the lives of my children, even since the womb, the sins and iniquity of my ancestors and all of their effects. I place the cross of Christ and the blood of Jesus between each generation of my family—between my parents and me, and between myself and my children, and every other generation going forward and declare that I and my descendants are free from every consequence of my ancestors' iniquity. Fill us with Your Spirit, God and heal the wounds of our hearts. In Jesus' mighty name, amen." [Further deliverance will be handled in the last chapter.]

---

[12] Google.com
[13] Google.com
[14] Google.com
[15] https://www.blueletterbible.org/lexicon/h6588/nkjv/wlc/0-1/
[16] https://www.blueletterbible.org/lexicon/h5771/nkjv/wlc/0-1/

10

DELIVERANCE FROM UNCLEAN SPIRITS

Crowds listened intently to Philip because they were eager to hear his message and see the miraculous signs he did. Many evil spirits were cast out, screaming as they left their victims.
(Acts 8:6-7 NLT)

Deliverance simply put is the silencing of and perhaps the eviction of demonic spirits from our mind, will, emotions or body that may be tormenting us in our thoughts, perhaps following us, attached to us or in us because of deeply rooted patterns of sin, lies of the enemy that we have been believing, traumatic experiences including others sinning against us, or iniquity passed on to us from our ancestors.[17] Manifestations of demons may happen in the physical body (as in the woman in the temple who was bent over for eighteen years from Luke 13:10-17) or may happen primarily in the mind which then can have a domino affect, touching other areas of who we are. In the case of the latter, we are speaking about *strongholds* of the mind (2 Cor. 10:4) which keep a person locked into a way of thinking that is wrong, skewed, exaggerated or twisted. A *stronghold* in the mind is a fortified neuropathway which is based on lies and defended by a demon of deception. I am using the term deliverance to describe freedom from demons in every area of our being.

The first debate I'd like to address is whether a Christian can have a demon affecting them in their soul (mind, will & emotions) or lodged in their body. It's normal to want to immediately and aggressively say, "No!" while grasping for a Bible verse to justify it because in all honesty, NO ONE wants to go *there*. And certainly, no one wants to be the one who has a demon, but a lot of people who struggle with demons behave, for the most part, normally. They're not presenting like the demoniac from the Gadarenes in Luke 8:26-33, ripping their clothes off and living in a graveyard. Instead, they're struggling internally with tormenting thoughts and impulses they are trying to suppress, or they're struggling to break out of a pattern of behavior or thinking that is not in line with God's purposes or plan.[18]

We like to think that when we get "saved" *everything* about us is *automatically* and *spontaneously* made new, but unfortunately, it's not. *Everything* is not made new in that one moment. No one has ever experienced complete transformation in spirit, soul, *and* body when they make a decision for Christ. We still have our earthly body after we get saved, don't we? We still battle against sickness after we get saved, don't we? We still struggle with sin habits like addictions and bad heart attitudes like unforgiveness after we get saved, right? We still need to have our mind renewed—in a sense re-programed—according to the Word of God, right?

Do Christians need deliverance? The answer, "No," is the tidy answer, but it's not the right answer. The right answer is, "Yes," because when we surrender to Christ and are saved, we are fully and completely healed and made whole in *spirit* only. The rest of us takes time. The rest of us takes a "laying it all down" and a surrendering of heart, mind, will, emotions, and desires, usually one piece at a time. Our soul is a complex, deep place where things get packed away and forgotten about. There are things still there that we don't even realize we never gave to God.

When that traumatic thing happened to you when you were nine, you didn't really understand it; all you really knew was that you felt confused, rejected and scared and all those feelings that didn't get processed got packed away into a tiny little box and stuffed down into your soul. Year after year, more little boxes got stacked on top of one another and stored away and before you realized it, you accepted the lies you heard from the *spirit of rejection.* You came into agreement with the lie that you were a reject, and that you would *always* be rejected and mistreated by those who were supposed to love you. Am I speaking to someone? This is only one scenario that invites a demon to live in us. There are so many more.

Unfortunately, we tend to act like hoarders when it comes to our heart and our emotions. We don't give things up easily and we are experts at trying to ignore and avoid pain.

We are a three-part being made in the image of God. We are primarily a spirit. We have a soul which consists of our mind, will, and emotions. And we live in a temporary physical *tent* which is our body. Because of the fall of Adam and Eve, every person that is born, is born dead to God and must be re-born by the Spirit to enter back into relationship with God. We do this by genuinely repenting for our sin, believing on the Lord Jesus Christ and being baptized. This is our born-again, salvation experience.

At the time that we are born again, it is our spirit that is born again, not our soul or our body. Our spirit is instantly re-born and renewed as the Holy Spirit takes up residence within us—our spirit and the Holy Spirit together in union, in our inner most being. It's a beautiful thing! We are *positionally* sanctified before God the Father. He accepts us just as we are as we become the righteousness of Christ, spiritually.

At the same time as we are born again *in spirit*, the *process* of sanctification in our soul begins. Second Corinthians 3:18 says:

> But we all, with unveiled face, beholding as in a mirror the glory of the Lord, *are being transformed into the same image from glory to glory*, just as by the Spirit of the Lord (NKJV, italics added).

Romans 12:2 says:

> And do not be conformed to this world [any longer with its superficial values and customs], but be transformed *and* progressively changed [as you mature spiritually] by the renewing of your mind [focusing on godly values and ethical attitudes], so that you may prove [for yourselves] what the will of God is, that which is good and acceptable and perfect [in His plan and purpose for you] (AMP).

The process of sanctification looks different for everyone, but it is a process of healing and refining that we lean into and invite the Holy Spirit to do. The speed of the process is very much determined by how we are willing to invite God in and allow the Holy Spirit to do what He wants to do. This process can also affect our body and cause it to manifest healing as our body will very often follow what happens in our mind, will, and emotions.[19] Part of this process is the deliverance from tormenting spirits that we have been talking about.

In the beginning, it was God's pleasure and desire to give us all free will so that we would love Him out of our own choice, not by some forced obligation. So, the human part of us, our soul, operates by free will; God has given *us* dominion over our own soul. We have the choice to submit to the Holy Spirit in our mind, will, and emotions and we have the choice not to. The Holy Spirit does not force Himself on us but waits for us to hand over to Him all we've held onto. We have a responsibility to partner with the Holy Spirit to bring about our own transformation by His power. Again, the verse from 1 Peter 5:8 begins, "Be sober, be vigilant..." and we know from elementary school that this type of statement called a "command" infers the pronoun "You" at the beginning. "(You) be sober, (You) be vigilant..." God is not going to do that part for you.

Sometimes a word picture or illustration helps us to understand difficult concepts. Let's consider the following illustration to help us understand how we can be oppressed by demons even though we're a Christian.

Imagine you lease a car. You don't own the car; it belongs to the car dealership, but it's on loan to you and you are responsible for its upkeep and maintenance. You drive the car anywhere you want and use it for whatever purpose your heart desires. You can also invite whomever you want, to ride along with you in the passenger seat.

Imagine also, that certain "less-desirable" passengers get to ride along with you *by default* based on the things that you do, participate in, carry forward from previous generations and don't let go of in your heart. These less-desirable passengers (demons) automatically get to ride with you, and they don't have to get out of the car until you stop giving them access, cut association with them and tell them to "get lost!"

You oversee that car on loan to you. You're responsible to take care of it. The owner of the car isn't responsible to put the right type of gas in the car; that's your job. The owner of the car isn't responsible to control who rides with you in the car. That's also your job! You are the one who opens and closes the door for your passengers according to your behavior, words, and the wounds in your heart which you try to ignore and don't tend to. You have the freedom to choose who and what you fellowship with. If you are abused but stuff the emotional trauma down in your soul rather than process it with the Lord, you open the door of your car to a spirit of abuse, trauma, perversion and a possible host of others (depending on what emotions you hold) which will ride with you for as long as you refuse to deal with your wound and command the demons to "Get out!"

Let's say you decide to believe on Jesus, and you become born-again. The Holy Spirit doesn't take over the whole car; He becomes a new engine for your car and occupies whatever other space you invite Him into. The Holy Spirit gives your car an oil change and becomes your new turbo-powered engine, but the car is still the same on the outside. Additionally, the passengers that are *already* in your car don't have to get out. They *only* get out when YOU stop giving them access (through your willingness to repent and take your wounds to God) and tell them to get out. The Holy Spirit doesn't force them out; He is required to allow you to call the shots in your soul realm. He does not overpower your free will. He's a gentleman and isn't into controlling you or forcing anything on you.

Are you getting the parallel here? Our body and soul are on loan to us from God. He created them and gave them to us to manage properly. When we don't do that, we pay the consequences.

Now, I hope there's a witness in your spirit that what I'm saying is truth. However, I do know there might be some still not convinced. Unfortunately, there is no scripture that explicitly says that a Christian can or can not have a demon and we don't explicitly see anyone being delivered from demons after they've entered the church. (Although this does not necessarily mean it didn't happen, just that it wasn't recorded.) However, there is one place where I can see that it could have happened and that is with Simon the sorcerer in Acts 8:5-24.

In Acts eight, Philip went to preach in Samaria, and the people were eager to hear what he had to say. The people responded favorably, and many believed and were baptized. Verse seven tells us that "many evil spirits were cast out, screaming as they left their victims" and many were healed from paralysis.

In that same town, there was a man named Simon who was a sorcerer, and he had amazed the local people with his magic. Verse thirteen tells us that even he believed Philip's message and was baptized. As a result, Simon began following Philip wherever he went. He was astonished by the signs and great miracles Philip performed. Let's look at verses 14-24 as follows:

> 14When the apostles in Jerusalem heard that the people of Samaria had accepted God's message, they sent Peter and John there. 15As soon as they arrived, they prayed for these new believers to receive the Holy Spirit. 16The Holy Spirit had not yet come upon any of them, for they had only been baptized in the name of the Lord Jesus. 17Then Peter and John laid their hands upon these believers, and they received the Holy Spirit. 18When Simon [the sorcerer] saw that the Spirit

> was given when the apostles laid their hands on people, he offered them money to buy this power. [19]"Let me have this power, too," he exclaimed, "so that when I lay my hands on people, they will receive the Holy Spirit!" [20]But Peter replied, "May your money be destroyed with you for thinking God's gift can be bought! [21]You can have no part in this, for your heart is not right with God. [22]Repent of your wickedness and pray to the Lord. Perhaps he will forgive your evil thoughts, [23]for I can see that you are full of bitter jealousy and are held captive by sin." [24]"Pray to the Lord for me," Simon exclaimed, "that these terrible things you've said won't happen to me!" (Acts 8:14-24 NLT, brackets added)

Verse thirteen explicitly says, "Then Simon himself believed and was baptized…" so we can't say, "Oh well, maybe he didn't really believe." No, if this were the case, it would not have been recorded as such. So how is it that Simon was "full of bitter jealousy and held captive to sin" after having believed and been baptized? Well, Simon was used to being paid to perform magic and he was simply continuing in what he knew—what was familiar. Simon had been operating in demonic power and was held captive in his mind to that way of doing things. He needed deliverance! Simon needed deliverance from bitterness, jealousy, and the demonic powers he agreed with as he performed magic. Unfortunately, the Bible does not record what happened after Simon asked Peter to pray. I think that Peter would have prayed with him and helped him to get free through repentance and deliverance, but unfortunately, we don't know for sure because it is not recorded.

I also believe that a possible reason why we don't see people in the Bible being delivered after joining the church is that the Apostles operated in their evangelistic anointing differently than *most* do today. They operated in great power and discernment. Demons could not hide from them. Deliverance, was therefore, something that happened at the moment of decision or baptism.

In the book of Acts, the Apostles very successfully followed the lead of the Holy Spirit when they preached the Gospel and brought people into the fellowship. It wasn't our westernized *short-cut* version that preaches a message and leads someone in a *sinner's prayer*. No! Deliverance and baptism were part of the original blueprint of conversion. Before anyone came into the church, their sin was turned away from, *and their demons were dealt with*. Everyone who was part of the church was expected to follow Christ's example of holiness, so they needed to be *cleaned up* and set free as much as possible to avoid getting tripped up or enticed back into sin.

The Apostles in the book of Acts did not simply preach Jesus and have people say a little prayer. The apostles in Acts preached in the power of the Holy Spirit, *immediately* baptized those who believed, in water *and* in the Holy Spirit, healed those who needed to be healed, and delivered those who needed to be delivered. They did not leave people demonized. In fact, they preached with such anointing and power that very often people were spontaneously delivered. We just saw this happening in Acts 8 when Philip preached in Samaria. Today, there are also pockets of evangelistic ministers doing this outside of the typical church. If you follow Kayla Gabbard on social media, you will see her baptizing people in the power of the Holy Spirit and *immediately* praying deliverance over them when they come out of the water. It's a beautiful thing. It doesn't happen in the local church because spontaneous baptism and deliverance isn't tidy and predictable. It can be messy, and it doesn't fit into the westernized church format.

This is the blueprint modeled by the apostles: make disciples by preaching, teaching, delivering, healing, and baptizing, all at the same outreach event. Unfortunately, very often we miss two out of five of these steps.

A large portion of the westernized church lacks power and doesn't operate in deliverance nor the gift of discerning of spirits. This gives us scores of Christians in the church who are still suffering with tormenting demonic spirits. No one has come along side them *in power* and helped them to be free. When they decided to believe and be baptized, deliverance was missed. And it would be easy to do that! It's not always obvious when someone has a demon. The demons tend to hide, plus, many oppressed people with physical manifestations are diagnosed by modern medicine, which conceals a spiritual problem as physical.

Having said all that, it is important to point out that one does not have to be delivered from demons in order to be saved. We see this in Mark, "He who believes and is baptized will be saved (Mark 16:16a NKJV). But in order to live for Christ in this world, experience peace, and be effective in our assignments and calling, we absolutely need to be delivered from demons. Deliverance is about our peace and effectiveness here and now on the earth. Because demons attach to the yet *unhealed* parts of our flesh, as soon as our body gives out and we cross over to be with Jesus forever, we become COMPLETELY healed and any demon that may still be hanging out with us has to leave to find another body/soul to occupy. The demon does NOT affect the location of our eternity.

We can be saved without deliverance, but we're not free on earth without it.

For clarity, I would like to also explain that Christians are not *possessed* by demons. Possession is about ownership and that term does not rightly describe how demons affect us. We are owned by Christ; we have been bought at a very high price (1 Cor. 6:20).

The original Greek word translated as *possessed,* in many biblical references, is *daimonízomai*. Daimonízomai does not mean *possession*. It means *to be under the power of a demon.*[20] A more accurate translation would therefore be *demonized* or possibly *oppressed*. Oppression is defined as *prolonged cruel or unjust treatment or control* and *mental pressure or distress*[21] which to me makes more sense. As a result, I always refer to being under the influence of a demon as being *oppressed*, *demonized,* or to *have a demon*.

Here's what the late Derek Prince, theologian and Bible teacher, who *was* one of the most reputable ministers of deliverance in his day, says in his book, *They Shall Expel Demons*, referring to Mark 1:23 which says, "Now there was a man in their synagogue *with an unclean spirit*" (NKJV):

> "In verse 23, when the NKJV says *with an unclean spirit*, the Greek actually says *in an unclean spirit*. Perhaps the nearest English equivalent would be *under the influence of an unclean spirit*.
>
> It is noteworthy that the New International Version translates this phrase *possessed by an evil spirit*. This exemplifies how translations can mislead us regarding the activity of evil spirits (or demons). Nothing in the original Greek justifies

> the use of the word *possessed*, with its suggestion of ownership. This translation is an accommodation to traditional religious terminology that obscures the meaning of the original text."[22]

In conclusion, *possessed* by an evil spirit is not an accurate translation. Sometimes going back to the original language clarifies the truth within the nuance of scripture.

Lastly, experience doesn't lie. I had been a Christian for over thirty years—a born-again Holy Spirit fired-up Christian, hearing the voice of God and operating in spiritual gifts, when I went for a deliverance appointment with a pastor I was studying under. I didn't think I needed it, but it was a requirement of my training. I thought I had surrendered the abuse from my earthly father to the Lord already, but as the pastor addressed it, I cried a lot of tears and accused my dad of being a monster. A demon of rage then manifested as my hands went up to my head grabbing my hair. I pulled at my hair as a roar came out of my mouth. The pastor cast that demon of rage out of me, and I crumbled back into tears, confessing the hatred and anger I had held on to. The struggle is real friends. Nothing demonic leaves us until we allow it to be exposed and release it to Jesus. Much of our "self-control" is pushing the demons down so they are not detected.

WHO IS DELIVERANCE FOR?

Deliverance is for anyone who will repent, turn to Jesus (make Him their Lord) and be baptized as the scriptures tell us to do. It is also for anyone who has already taken these steps in obedience, at anytime. It is not something that *needs* to be done immediately or within the first few months of being a believer; it's better that way but deliverance can be done anytime. Also, it may not be something that happens all in one shot. Very often, people are healed and delivered in stages; it seems that over time as a person matures spiritually, the demon loses its ability to hide and stay. As well, it also depends on the level of anointing in operation around us. When we avail ourselves to church gatherings where the power of the Holy Spirit is honored and invited to come, and worship has prepared the atmosphere, very often deliverance happens spontaneously. This happened to me many years ago while attending my first conference with Apostle Barbara Yoder's ministry.

It was a very large 2-day gathering at the Sheraton hotel near the Detroit airport. Many anointed ministers were speaking over the course of the conference, and I benefited greatly from what they brought into the room. A man by the name of Trevor Baker from the UK spoke in the afternoon and as he talked about the unclean spirit called the *orphan spirit* which keeps us trapped in an orphan mentality and out of sonship with Father God, I began to manifest in my seat. It wasn't super dramatic, but it was obvious to those directly around me that God was delivering me. The lovely woman next to me, whom I had just met, gently put her hand on me and prayed. It was a bit embarrassing, but I focused on being grateful that the Lord had set me free instead of worrying about what other people thought. Honestly, I expect most people in that meeting were used to seeing stuff like that. I had never heard of the orphan spirit nor was I aware it had been affecting me. But hallelujah for freedom. I'm all for it, regardless of what it looks like.

Deliverance very often accompanies deep healing or what some might call inner-healing or emotional healing. This is the healing of emotional wounds and the lies that we believe associated with the trauma we may have endured. As the foothold that the demon is using is removed, the demon leaves because there's no longer a legal right for it to stay.

The demon loses its grip when what it has been feasting on is healed.

Jesus told us in Luke 11:24-26:

> "When an impure spirit comes out of a person, it goes through arid places seeking rest and does not find it. Then it says, 'I will return to the house I left.' When it arrives, it finds the house swept clean and put in order. Then it goes and takes seven other spirits more wicked than itself, and they go in and live there. And the final condition of that person is worse than the first" (NIV).

We learn from this that it is very important for us to be filled with the Holy Spirit afresh after deliverance. Any place that has been vacated must be filled by the Spirit. Afterall, scripture does tell us to be *continually* filled with the Spirit.

Ephesians 5:18 says, "Do not get drunk on wine, which leads to debauchery. Instead, be filled with the Spirit" (NIV). The phrase *be filled* was translated from a Greek verb in the *present perfect* tense which according to Chuck Smith's commentary on Blueletterbible.org indicates a continual filling, not a one-time occurrence.[23] This is further understood when we consider that Jesus described the presence of the Spirit within, to the woman at the well in John 7:38, as *rivers of living water*. Rivers flow. They are not stagnant bodies of water like wells, but one that continually flows in and out requiring an inlet that does not cease supplying the water.

HOW DO WE BECOME DEMONIZED?

Oppression from demons can occur due to traumatic wounds inflicted upon our soul because of abuse or any other traumatic event. As well, demons, called familiar spirits can be passed onto us from our ancestors due to deeply rooted patterns of sin (iniquity) causing us to have a "bent" toward a particular type of sin. This is why addictions and other things like certain infirmities, diseases, and behaviors *run* in families—they are said to be *genetic*. We are predisposed to certain things from our ancestors. The area of sexual dysfunction, lust, and perversion is one of those areas that is seen as *running* in families. It is, therefore, very important to confess the sexual sins of our ancestors and cut them off with the blood of Jesus so they are not passed on. We should have already done that back in the previous chapter on *Stewarding Our Family Line*.

HOW DO WE GET FREE?

Well, there are ministers that specialize in deliverance, but you do want to be careful who you randomly trust in this area. You want to know exactly who you are trusting with this ministry in your life. The good news is much can be accomplished in your own prayer life, and you *can* cast demons out of yourself if you know they are there, but you do have to do the groundwork first. What groundwork? The groundwork we have been doing all throughout this book, namely the following:

- repenting for and renouncing our own sin;
- renouncing shame and fear;
- breaking soul-ties;
- confessing our traumatic experiences to the Lord and all the associated feelings we have stuffed and hidden;
- repenting for and renouncing the reactive sin we have engaged in like anger, hate, unforgiveness, bitterness, judgements, and inner vows we took associated with people sinning against us;
- breaking any other vows we took in error;
- repenting for erroneously blaming God for our pain;

- and confessing and renouncing the iniquity in our bloodline for the sin of previous generations.

If you have not completed all the previous exercises and prayers, please go back and to the best of your ability, join your heart and faith to the prayers offered. Repentance and renunciation must be complete before attempting to deal with demons that may be associated with our sin and iniquity.

Let's continue in the next chapter.

---

[17]Iniquity is *not* the same as sin. Iniquity is the propensity or bent to sin a certain way that has been passed down from previous generations (see Ex. 20:5, Ex. 34:7, Num. 14:18, Deut. 5:9).

[18] Remember what Jesus said to Peter in Matthew 16:23? "Get behind Me, Satan! You are an offense to Me, for you are not mindful of the things of God, but the things of men (NKJV). Peter was being deceived in his mind about the will of God.

[19]Proverbs 17:22, "A happy heart is good medicine and a joyful mind causes healing, But a broken spirit dries up the bones" (AMP).

[20]https://www.blueletterbible.org/lexicon/g1139/kjv/tr/0-1/

[21]Google dictionary

[22]Derek Prince, *They Shall Expel Demons: What You Need to Know about Demons—Your Invisible Enemies* (Bloomington: Chosen Books, 1998, 2020) 25. Print.

[23]www.blueletterbible.org/Comm/smith_chuck/c2000_Eph/Eph_005.cfm?a=1102018

11

HOW TO PRAY DELIVERANCE OVER YOURSELF

So submit to [the authority of] God. Resist the devil [stand firm against him] and he will flee from you. (James 4:7 AMP)

Once we have submitted to God by confessing, repenting, and renouncing, we come against, resist, bind and command demons to go in Jesus' name. To renounce means to divorce, completely turn against, abandon, and reject. To bind means to wrap in chains and restrict. Jesus said in Matthew 16:19 the following:

> I will give you the keys (authority) of the kingdom of heaven; and whatever you bind [forbid, declare to be improper and unlawful] on earth will have [already] been bound in heaven, and whatever you loose [permit, declare lawful] on earth will have [already] been loosed in heaven. (AMP)

We, who are born-again, spiritual, and discerning in the Spirit, align the governance of ourselves with heaven, by commanding spirits to be bound and loosed according to *heaven's* agenda. We know that it is *not* the will of God for us to be influenced or harassed by demons. So, we bind demonic spirits to restrict them and forbid them from manifesting, and we loose the Holy Spirit (or whatever facet of the Holy Spirit[24] we need) to assist us in our circumstances and assignments.

Here's a question some may be asking themselves: *Can't I just skip this last step of deliverance? I don't feel like I have demons.* You can skip this step if you want to, but I do not recommend it as you will continue to be harassed with temptation, possibly beyond your ability to resist. You will not be completely free without deliverance. It's common not to feel like you need deliverance. Demons tend to hide. But they show up when we're asleep, stressed, distracted, or weary and tired. The assault in our thoughts can be overwhelming so don't leave yourself subject to their harassment.

We will not be dealing with occult level demons in our prayer; as I have said previously, if you were a victim of SRA, please see a professional who is familiar with this type of bondage and deliverance.

We will be dealing with five main strongman demons. They are the spirit of perversion (Is. 19:14), the spirit of harlotry (Hosea 1:2, Hosea 4:12), the spirit of fear (2 Timothy 1:7), the spirit of heaviness (Is. 61:3), and the spirit of bondage (Romans 8:15 & Gal. 5:1).

The spirit of perversion is the twisting of truth or of what God created. Harlotry is not in the sense that we think of it. You may assume that because you have not sold your body, it's not something that affects you, but harlotry is the spirit behind idolatry—turning away from God and seeking lesser lovers to meet your needs. Hosea 1:2 says, "When the LORD began to speak by Hosea, the LORD said to Hosea: "Go, take yourself a wife of harlotry and children of harlotry, for the land has committed great harlotry by departing from the LORD."

Have you ever been in a relationship that the Lord clearly did not approve of? Have you ever chosen that person above your relationship with Jesus? If the Lord is not your number One, your first love, and the most important love of your life, you are partnering with a spirit of harlotry.

Bondage is slavery. If you have struggled to stop a certain sin but haven't been able to, you are being controlled by a spirit of bondage.

This is the point where our pride can hinder our deliverance. Please pray and seek the Lord before you assume you are not under the influence of these demons. Again, the ruling spirits are perversion, harlotry, fear, heaviness, and bondage.

Under these strongman spirits are a host of demons which may include the following:

> Self-protection, pride, hard-heartedness, cold-heartedness, lust, frigidity, anger, rage, violence, unforgiveness, hate, bitterness, judgement, deception, depression, confusion, grief, despair, anxiety, idolatry, abuse, victimization, addiction, self-hate, self-rejection, self-harm, control, lying, strife, chaos, fear of rejection, fear of abuse, fear of punishment, fear of shame, fear of people, fornication, self-gratification, sodomy, incest, pornography, homosexuality, transgenderism, gender dysphoria, adultery, and every other kind of deviant sexual desire.

Please go before the Lord in prayer and ask Him to show you what you need to kick out from the list above or just kick them all out.

As we pray through deliverance, if you have not previously repented and renounced certain behaviors connected to a demon, don't attempt to kick the demon out yet. If the Holy Spirit has convicted you of one of the above things, repent for it and renounce it FIRST (if you haven't done so already). Receive the forgiveness and cleansing of the Lord and then bind the demon and tell it to go, in Jesus' name. Consider revisiting portions of the book if it has been a long time since you have worked through it.

FEAR, ANXIETY, WORRY, AND HEAVINESS

2 Timothy 1:7 says, "For God has not given us a spirit of fear, but of power and of love and of a sound mind." Being fearful of not praying through everything correctly or missing some aspect of your deliverance or being fearful to pray against demons is not of God. If this is you, you are missing the revelation of the amazing power, scope, and magnitude of God's mercy and grace. We are doing our part by praying and God is doing His part by covering us when we're not perfect. We need to trust Him through this whole process. As I said earlier, the Lord wants us to be delivered and to be whole; He is doing and will do everything in His power to make it so.

Being fearful of being deceived is also not of God. No type of fear except the "fear of God" (which isn't really fear), is from God. The "fear of God" is reverence, an understanding of and respect for His power, might, and holiness.

Anxiety is the fear of the unknown, fear of the future or the fear of bad things happening in the future. This is also not from God because God is good and He takes everything that happens in our lives and turns it around for our good (Romans 8:28). He has also promised to never leave us or forsake us. He walks with us and carries us through difficult circumstances. Isaiah 41:10 says, "Fear not, for I *am* with you; Be not dismayed, for I *am* your God. I will strengthen you, yes, I will help you, I will uphold you with My righteous right hand." Proverbs 12:25 says, "Anxiety in the heart of man causes depression, but a good word makes it glad."

Worry… not of God. In John 14:27 Jesus says, "Peace I leave with you; my peace I give you. I do not give to you as the world gives. Do not let your hearts be troubled (worried) and do not be afraid" (NIV, brackets mine). Psalms 55:22, "Cast your burden on the LORD [release it] and He will sustain *and* uphold you; He will never allow the righteous to be shaken (slip, fall, fail)" (AMP). 1 Peter 5:6-7 says, "Therefore humble yourselves under the mighty hand of God, that He may exalt you in due time, casting all your care upon Him, for He cares for you."

Isaiah 61:1-3 says the following:

> "The Spirit of the Lord GOD *is* upon Me, because the LORD has anointed Me to preach good tidings to the poor; He has sent Me to heal the brokenhearted, to proclaim liberty to the captives, and the opening of the prison to *those who are* bound; to proclaim the acceptable year of the LORD, and the day of vengeance of our God; to comfort all who mourn, to console those who mourn in Zion, to give them beauty for ashes, the oil of joy for mourning, the garment of praise for the *spirit of heaviness*; that they may be called trees of righteousness, the planting of the LORD, that He may be glorified" (emphasis added).

Heaviness is a spirit and is cast off by choosing to enter into praise instead. Heaviness is like a cloak put around your shoulders when you choose to partner with fear, anxiety, and worry. Jesus said in Matthew 11:28-30 the following:

> Come to Me, all *you* who labor and are heavy laden, and I will give you rest. Take My yoke upon you and learn from Me, for I am gentle and lowly in heart, and you will find rest for your souls. For My yoke *is* easy and My burden is light."

There is no heavy burden you are meant to carry. If you've been trying to carry a burden, give it to Jesus and take His yoke... His burden... instead. It is time to finally come out of agreement with fear, anxiety, worry, and heaviness. Let's do that now together.

PRAYER

> "Lord God, I come to You in my weariness and heaviness, and I ask You to set me free. I confess to You, God, that I have agreed with fear. I have been afraid of ... *[name what you have been afraid of]*. I confess that I have partnered with anxiety and allowed it to control my thinking. I have been worried about the future and fearful of bad things happening to me and my family. I have been waiting for the shoe to drop, and I know that is not of you. I have agreed with the expectation of negativity, trauma, and loss. This does not line up with your Word or heart for me, and I am sorry. I have not given all my burdens and cares to You; I have tried to carry them alone; I have been prideful, and I have been foolish because this is beyond my capability and power. I repent. Lord, I confess that my family and my ancestors have also operated in fear, anxiety, worry, and have been burdened by heaviness. I ask You, God, to forgive my ancestors and I. We have not heeded Your

Word, and we have not been wise. Please forgive us. Lord, I submit to you now. And I choose to forgive myself and my ancestors for our disobedience to Your direction for our lives. I receive Your forgiveness in full and thank You for it, in Jesus' name. Lord, I give You the burdens of my heart. I give You my future. I give You my finances. I give You my job (or job situation). I give You my co-workers and my boss/employees. I give You my living situation. I give You my friends. I give You my family (mother/father/siblings). I give You my children (if applicable). I give You my marriage (if applicable) and I ask You, God, to be in control of it all. Heal the wounds of my heart, God, that have caused me to be in this state of mind. Heal the disappointments of my past and help me to see how You have redeemed them and brought good out of them. I believe that You are good, Lord, and I believe that You are working on my behalf. I believe, God, that You are for me and not against me, always.

In the name of Jesus, I take authority over fear, anxiety, worry, and heaviness, and I command them to untangle and untie from one another right now; they will stop reinforcing one another right now. In Jesus' name, I bind fear, anxiety, worry, and heaviness right now and I restrict their maneuvers against me and say they will not cause me harm in any way. In Jesus' name, I command fear, anxiety, worry, and heaviness to leave me now upon my natural breathing. You will not cause me harm. Fear, anxiety, worry, and heaviness, you will come up and out now, in Jesus' name. Go to the feet of Jesus and never come back.

All fear, anxiety, worry and heaviness are leaving me now, in Jesus' name. Thank You, Lord. *[breathe deep and by faith know that these spirits are leaving.]*

Lord, I ask You to cleanse my blood and my bloodline up through the generations and down to my descendants. I place the cross of Christ between my parents and I, and between me and my descendants, and declare every curse is broken, in Jesus' name. The members of my family, in the power of Christ, will no longer agree with fear, anxiety, worry, or heaviness. We will rely on the Lord and cease expecting negative outcomes. We trust in the goodness of God to bring favor, rest, and restoration to us in every way. Show me Lord, how to bring my actions and my everyday words into agreement with Your will for my life. I command every word curse I have spoken, every negative word I have spoken about myself, my ancestors, my descendants, my marriage, my family, and my future to be broken now… to fall to the ground fruitless, in Jesus' name. Forgive me God for speaking negatively about these things. I now choose to be joyful and to praise Your name, O God, even when things don't happen the way I want them to. I lift Your name up, God. I give You praise. And I give You thanks. Holy Spirit fill me full with Your abiding presence. Don't leave any place in me vacant but be my Helper and my ever-present Peace, living in me. In Jesus' mighty name, amen.

THE UNCLEAN SPIRIT OF LYING

One area the Lord is bringing to my mind right now is lying… not walking in truth. The belt in the armor of God represents truth. If we are not walking in truth… meaning we are either lying to ourselves, lying to God, or lying to others or we are trying to hide something from someone, we are not wearing the belt of truth. We must understand that truth is part of our foundation; Jesus is truth and He is our foundation. Truth sets us free.

Now, if you lie to someone so you can throw them a surprise party, that's okay, because your heart is not lying with an evil intention. The issue is the intent of the heart. And I would say, with 99% of lies, there is ungodly intentions or needs at work. I think most people lie to protect themselves—to avoid punishment, exposure, accountability, responsibility, or being hurt by others whether there is a real threat or not. So, the true issue then is avoidance. What are we trying to avoid by lying? Sometimes we avoid the godly action we need to take because of fear—the fear of the unknown, the fear of people, the fear of being hurt, fear of being alone, fear of rejection, fear of financial lack, the fear of people's opinions and what they will think of us, fear of judgement, and more. We really need to understand why we are lying AND whether there is some other godly action we need to take so we stop lying, like removing ourselves from toxic relationships or trusting God as we finally stand up for ourselves and have that difficult conversation.

If someone gets up in the morning and in their devotion time with God, prays a prayer to put on the belt of truth but then lies to a friend about their availability that day because they don't want to spend time with them, they have in effect taken the belt of truth off; they are no longer wearing it. We fool ourselves into thinking it's okay to lie in these cases because we don't want to hurt someone's feelings. But in reality, we are avoiding the truth because we don't know how to have an honest conversation without hurting them.

(Perhaps we are partnering with the fear of man or the fear of hurting someone's feelings... or maybe we are just limited in our communication skills. We must discern in the power of the Holy Spirit.) No matter what, our actions and words must line up with what the armor of God represents.

To wear the belt of truth, we need to be truthful. Do not be deceived! We are not allowed to be hypocritical. The devil is the *father* of lies (John 8:44) and every time we lie or misrepresent ourselves (to ourselves or others), we align with the devil which undermines our authority. We say we aren't angry but deep down we are! We are not being truthful with ourselves. In this case, we could have trouble kicking the devil out; we can't tell demons to go in one area while still being in the devil's camp in another. We may not be able to get free from hatred if we haven't repented for and renounced the spirit of lying. And this is true for other things as well; we may have trouble getting free from lust if we're still offended by something our husband said, did or didn't do. We will have trouble getting free from anything if we're still holding onto anger about something else. We must allow the Holy Spirit to search our heart and convict us. I pray you get what I am saying *without* getting into fear. Pray my friend! Ask the Holy Spirit to search your heart and be willing to agree with what He shows you. Then repent.

Let's pray about lying and kick it out.

PRAYER

> "Lord God, I repent for lying—for not telling the truth and for not walking in complete honesty with myself, You, and others. I have not been completely aware of what is truly in my heart, and I am sorry. I have said that I'm not angry when truly I am. I have said that I forgive when truly I haven't. Please forgive me for speaking empty

words—words that I have not agreed with in my heart. I repent for lying to You. I repent for lying to myself. And I repent for lying to others all in an attempt to avoid ... *[name what you were avoiding]*. Forgive me, God, for harboring anger and for not being truthful about it. I repent. And I receive Your forgiveness and cleansing. I receive Your forgiveness for lying and not walking in complete truth. Cleanse me, God.

I forgive myself and I forgive all others who have lied to me. I completely renounce lying and deception and I divorce myself from that spirit now, in Jesus' mighty name. In the authority Jesus has given me, I bind and break the power of the lying spirit and the spirit of deception, and I command these demons to leave me now, in Jesus' name. Lying and deception, you will cease your maneuvers against me; you will shut your mouth; and you will stop harassing me and speaking in my mind, now, in Jesus' name. I put a gag order on you now, in Jesus' name. You are bound and restricted from operating, and you will leave me now. Go to the feet of Jesus and never come back. Get out and get off of me! Your rights have been stripped. Leave me now, in Jesus' name. *[Breathe deep and blow it out.]*

Thank You, God. Thank You, Jesus. Thank You, Holy Spirit. Thank You that it is done; it is finished. It is done! And it is finished! I lift You up, God, and glorify Your name. You are on the throne of my heart. Come, Holy Spirit! Fill me up with Your goodness, Your peace, Your Glory, Your Presence, and Your power. Saturate me

> afresh. I love You. You are my everything. You are all I need. In Jesus' name, amen.

If you need to, repeat the prayers until you can say them with conviction, authority, and power.

ONE LAST REVIEW OF SEXUAL SIN

Okay friends, before we pray our final deliverance prayer, I'd like you to do one last review of what sexual practices are sin according to the Holy Spirit. I invited you to read through a list of scriptures back in the chapter, *Square One*. Because the Lord wants you to be free and because the curriculum in the public schools changed back in 2015, introducing students to all kinds of sexually perverted acts, teaching them as if they were common and acceptable, I'd like you to go to prayer and ask the Lord specifically if the following things are acceptable to Him: oral sex, annal sex (sodomy), masturbation/self-gratification (with or without toys) and viewing pornography. I'm not asking you to give your opinion. I'm not asking you to regurgitate what you've been taught or what works for you. I'm asking you to ask the Lord, WITHOUT BIAS. So, first, we need to become *unbiased* in our opinion because if we have a strong opinion, it can very easily distort what we discern. We must be willing to give up whatever the Lord says is not godly… whatever that looks like and whatever that means for us and for our marriage.

So, what from the above list do you have a strong opinion of? What would you not be willing to give up? Okay. Why? Why are you not willing to give it up? Now ask God if your answer to the question, "Why?" is true or if your reasoning is twisted. God created sex to be enjoyed in the confines of marriage between a man and a woman… one person with a penis and one person with a vagina because one fits into the other. Any deviation from this is not of God. Can you see that? The devil is the twister of everything divine. He takes literally everything God has created and twists it into something deviant.

If we do not repent for something we have been doing which is not holy, we will not be free. We will leave room for the devil to continue to harass us.

If God has convicted you of something, please take the time now to repent and renounce that activity. Then trust God with the results and the outcome. Trust God to enrich your sex life according to His plan and purpose—to cause you to enjoy what He created, His way. Once you go through the final deliverance prayer below, you will find it easier to do that.

FINAL DELIVERANCE

Okay, let's continue with our final deliverance from the spirits we have been contending with throughout the main portions of this book.

Because in our prayers, we are binding demons first, there should not be any extreme manifestations. You may yawn, cough, cry or even burp, but if there is no physical indication of demons leaving, I always encourage people to believe *in faith* that the demons are leaving upon their natural breathing. You can purposely blow out of your mouth, if you want to join an action to your faith. In Luke 10:19 Jesus says, "Behold, I give you the authority to trample on serpents and scorpions, and over all the power of the enemy, and nothing shall by any means hurt you." If Jesus said it, we need to believe it.

You may wonder, *are you saying I might be possessed?* No. I'm not saying you're possessed. I'm saying you may be oppressed, which means your behavior or your thinking is being influenced by demons. Is the demon inside you or outside? It doesn't really matter because you can get rid of it either way. But if the demon is inside you, you will be controlled by it at a much greater level and you may even have "black out" moments when you don't remember what happened or moments when you feel like you are standing outside your body watching yourself do and say things without being able to control it. (I've not personally had these experiences, but I've heard about others having them.) Even so, remember who you are! And whose you are! Declare Who God is, submit yourself to God, confess, repent, renounce, plead the blood of Jesus over yourself, declare who you are in Christ, bind the demons, and kick them out.

If you feel afraid or intimated in any way, get some help. It's not uncommon for a demon of intimidation to operate and make you nervous to do what Jesus has equipped you to do. The devil is a liar! You are equipped with His power and authority to stand against the darkness. Make sure you are confident and able to proceed in faith before you go further by yourself.

PRAYER

> "Father God, thank You for Who You are on my behalf. Thank You that You are my fierce Defender and Protector. You are my rock, my shield, my fortress, and strong tower. I run into You and am safe.[25] Thank You for Your mercy, grace, forgiveness, and love. Cover me God. Hide me in You. Thank You, God, that You surround me with songs of deliverance. Deliver me, God. I look to You for help. Thank You for Your Son, Jesus, Who died for me—Who made a way for me to be fully accepted and forgiven by You, God.

[If applicable] Lord God, I confess that I have been cold toward my husband. I have tried to avoid sexual intimacy with him because of my wounds and a distorted view of sex and I am sorry. I know that sex is part of marriage and it is godly for us to enjoy it together. I repent. I choose to forgive *[your husband's name]* for ... *[name anything that he has done or said that has bothered you or hurt you as it relates to sex]*. I choose to let it go. Help me, Jesus. Heal the wounds of my heart in this area, God.

Lord, I confess that I have turned my affections away from You and toward other things at times and I am sorry. There have been things that I have not wanted to give up to follow Your ways and to love You as I should, and I am sorry.

I have confessed my sin to You and turned away from it. [If there is something you still need to confess, do it now: Lord, I confess *(fill in the blank)* I repent and turn away from it. Please forgive me. I receive Your forgiveness. I renounce *(same thing you just confessed)* and I break my agreement with it now, in Jesus' name.]

I have forgiven myself, my husband, and all who perpetrated sin against me and treated me unjustly. Lord, if there is anyone I still need to forgive, put them on my heart now. *[Wait on the Lord.]*

I declare that the blood of Jesus covers me and my home and my family. In Your strength and enabling, God, I have put on truth by being truthful and believing truth. I have put on righteousness by putting my full trust in Jesus and His sacrifice and not taking advantage of grace by doing whatever I want; I have submitted my entire life to the

Lordship of Christ. In Your strength, God, I have shod my feet in peace by believing the full gospel of Jesus Christ. I have put on faith and salvation by repenting and submitting my life to Christ. Because of You, I am well prepared with the armor of God. According to Your Word, God, in Luke 10:19, I have been given authority over ALL the power of the enemy; nothing shall by any means hurt me and I believe You. According to 1 John 5:18, anyone born of God does not continue to habitually sin; the One who was born of God—Jesus, keeps me safe, and the evil one cannot harm me. So, I submit to you, Lord; I rest in Your protection, and I trust in Your mercy. I declare that I am a daughter of God who has been purchased by the blood of Jesus, fully redeemed, cleansed, and forgiven by Him. I possess all the rights of an heir to the Kingdom of God. The devil has no ground in me.

In the authority of Jesus Christ, I loose the Holy Sprit and the host of angel armies my Father has assigned to me, right now, to assist in my deliverance. I confess and repent for partnering with perversion *[the twisting of truth]*, harlotry[26], fear, heaviness, and bondage. Please forgive me, God."

Renounce, bind and break strongman demons: "And in the name of Jesus Christ, I renounce, bind, and break the power of perversion, harlotry, fear, heaviness, and bondage."

Renounce, bind and break all other lower-level demons: "In the name of Jesus, I renounce, bind, and break the power of … [*speak all you have repented of or experienced:* self-protection, pride, hard-heartedness, cold-heartedness, lust, frigidity, anger, rage, violence, unforgiveness, hate, bitterness, offense, judgement, deception, depression, confusion, grief, despair, anxiety, idolatry, abuse, victimization, addiction, self-hate, self-rejection, self-harm, control, lying, strife, chaos, fear of rejection, fear of abuse, fear of punishment, fear of shame, fear of people, fornication, self-gratification, sodomy, incest, pornography, homosexuality, trans-genderism, gender dysphoria, adultery, rape) and every unclean sexual desire.

Not one of these demons shall cause me grief or harm in any way. In Jesus' name, they are bound and they are restricted from operating against me."

Cast out: "In Jesus' name, I command ... [*speak all you have bound and renounced above:* self-protection, pride, hard-heartedness, cold-heartedness, lust, frigidity, anger, rage, violence, unforgiveness, hate, bitterness, offense, judgement, deception, depression, confusion, grief, despair, anxiety, idolatry, abuse, victimization, addiction, self-hate, self-rejection, self-harm, control, lying, strife, chaos, fear of rejection, fear of abuse, fear of punishment, fear of shame, fear of people, fornication, self-gratification, sodomy, incest, pornography, homosexuality, trans-genderism, gender dysphoria, adultery, rape) and every unclean sexual desire to leave me now. Go. Get out, in Jesus' name. Come up and out in Jesus' name. Go to the feet of Jesus. Now! I cancel my agreements with you. Go now. *[keep commanding these demons to leave until you have a sense that they have gone. You can speak the name individually if you have to.]*

And in Jesus' name, I command perversity, harlotry, fear, heaviness, and bondage to leave me now. Come up and out in Jesus' name! You cannot stay. You must go, now! Go now. Up and out, in Jesus' name.

[Allow yourself to do what you need to do; if it's coughing, let it happen. Keep commanding the demons to leave until you sense the Holy Spirit telling you it's done. You may not have any physical symptoms which is totally fine. Simply breathe deep and exhale believing in faith that they are leaving on your breath.]

Go now! I am a daughter of King Jesus, and you have no right to stay or harass me. Leave me now. I am covered in the blood of Jesus. I am protected. I am His. Perversion, go, in Jesus' name! Bondage, go! Harlotry, go!

[Continue on as you are led until you are free. Believe in your authority. Don't be passive about it. Command spirits to leave like you mean it—like you have the authority to do it, because you do. If you begin to have a physical manifestation like coughing or getting emotional, take that as a sign that these spirits are dislodging and beginning to move; keep commanding things up and out.]

In Jesus' name, I decree that I am free and I break every curse these demons were assigned to carry out. Every curse is broken by the blood of Jesus. The curse against my marriage is broken. The curse against my sexuality is broken. I decree that I am free to be all God created me to be, and to do all God has for me to do. Whomever the Son sets free is free indeed and that includes me! I decree that goodness and mercy is following me and will follow me all the days of my life and I will dwell in safety in the house of the Lord forever (Psalm 23:6).

[Consider taking communion. Pray: "On the night He was betrayed, Jesus took bread, gave thanks to God, and gave it to His disciples saying, 'This is my body which is given for you. Do this in remembrance of me.' Thank You, God, for this bread/cracker which represents the broken body of Your Son, Jesus. Thank You that His body was broken for my healing and as I eat His body, eternal life is made manifest in mine. As I partake, I remember and honor His sacrifice. I live because He lives *[break the cracker and partake]*."

Take your juice and pray: "Also on the night He was betrayed, Jesus took a cup and said, 'This cup is the new covenant between God and his people—an agreement confirmed with my blood, which is poured out as a sacrifice for you." Thank You, God, for this wine/juice which represents Your blood poured out for me for the forgiveness of my sins, sealing our covenantal promise together. As I partake, putting my faith behind my action, may Your blood wash me clean. *[Partake of the juice/wine.]* Thank You, Lord. I bless You and worship You with all that I am. Amen."]

Continue:

Hallelujah! Thank You, Jesus. Holy Spirit, fill me afresh with Your power and presence. Baptize me again! Fill every place that was vacated and fill me

> to overflowing. Saturate me, Holy Spirit. I invite You to be my all in all.
>
> *[Let the Holy Spirit fill you. Sit in it for a few minutes and worship Him. Consider listening to Holy Spirit / The Dove by SEU Worship with Chelsea Plank or another worship song about the Holy Spirit.]*
>
> Fill me, God, with Your presence. I need You. I need all of You. Thank You, God, my Great Deliverer.
>
> In Your most holy name, Jesus, amen."

In case you need suggestions, other worship songs that will minister to you and invite God's presence are: *All of You or Nothing* by GPA Worship, *First Love* by Kari Jobe Carnes, *Healing in His Wounds* by GPA Worship featuring Carys Rimmer, *Fall Like Rain* by Passion and Kari Jobe Carnes, and *Give Me Oil* by Jesus Image.

Once you have prayed through all the issues and prayed deliverance over yourself, if you sense you're still not free, you will need to find someone who will come alongside you and help you discern. We must be able to discern the leading of the Lord and know when the enemy is trying to confuse us or lie to us, and we need to be careful not to give the devil anymore airtime or attention than is necessary. After praying through, focus your attention on the Lord and His goodness and rest in Him. Do not allow the enemy to get you into a spiral of fear, worry, and anxiety over whether or not you are free. James 4:7 says, *"Therefore submit to God. Resist the devil and he will flee…"* This is the Word of God. Do you believe it? Yes? Did you submit to God? Yes? Did you resist the devil? Yes? Then the devil has no choice but to flee. Stand on the Word of God. The Lord is with you! He has not left you alone to figure this out by yourself. Rest in Him. Trust Him. Listen for His voice.

If you need to, pray the following again:

> "I repent for being in fear, anxiety, and worry. I renounce fear, anxiety, and worry and I command every voice of fear, anxiety, and worry to be silent now, in Jesus' name. I command fear, anxiety, and worry to leave me now; go to the feat of Jesus and never come back, in Jesus' name. I thank You, God, that I am Yours and that You are on the throne of my life. You, Lord, are my rock and my hiding place. Surround me, God, in Your love and Your peace. Fill me, Holy Spirit, completely full with Your abiding presence and power. Come and saturate me in You. In Jesus' name, amen."

As a further declaration, you can read Psalm 91 over yourself.

MAINTAINING YOUR DELIVERANCE

Finally, after we have done so much work uprooting all the painful memories and praying through, let's make sure we don't fall back into sin. Falling back into sin will get us in trouble again, so ask the Lord what you need to stay away from, to avoid temptation and re-verting back to torment. For myself, I need to abstain from any show or movie with explicit sex scenes. I find that if I watch them, I start having dreams I don't want to have again, and I need to repent all over again. So, know what your triggers are. Know where the enemy gets you tripped up and tempts you. Some other suggestions are the following:

- Clean up your Facebook feed from smut and garbage; unfollow, unfriend, hide, and block what you need to.

- Stop hanging out with friends that talk about inappropriate things or gossip.
- Burn the books that tempt you into sexual fantasy.
- Forgive your husband daily for not meeting your needs or being too grabby or struggling with lust himself. Pray for him… that he would be convicted and get the help he needs in this same area.
- When you're in prayer, take your husband's sin to the foot of the cross as well as yours; you are in covenant with him which makes you one. So, confess his sin as if it's yours. Trust me! It works.
- Pray every night before sleep for the Spirit to control your dreams and declare who you are in Him. State that nothing evil is allowed to operate around you during the night season.
- Anoint your bed and your pillow with oil representing the Holy Spirit.
- Repent for any sin that may have occurred in your room by you or a previous occupant.
- Cleanse the room of any evil spirits by commanding them to leave in Jesus' name.
- Anoint your door and window to seal it shut from intruders. But don't do any of it out of fear but in an understanding of stewardship and authority.
- Get into community with like-minded, Spirit-filled, believing women for support.
- Love people just like Jesus loved people, in purity of heart, and perfect intentions but use godly wisdom. Not every person knows how to take, respond to, or recognize godly love in action.
- Pray and pursue the Lord. Love Him with all your heart, with all your soul, and with all your mind, then love your neighbor as yourself.
- Abide in the true vine.

- Read Psalm 91 out loud over yourself, your family, and your home.

He who dwells in the secret place of the Most High shall abide under the shadow of the Almighty. I will say of the LORD, "*He is* my refuge and my fortress; my God, in Him I will trust." Surely He shall deliver you from the snare of the fowler *and* from the perilous pestilence. He shall cover you with His feathers, and under His wings you shall take refuge; His truth *shall be your* shield and buckler. You shall not be afraid of the terror by night, *nor* of the arrow *that* flies by day, *nor* of the pestilence *that* walks in darkness, *nor* the destruction *that* lays waste at noonday. A thousand may fall at your side, and ten thousand at your right hand; *But* it shall not come near you. Only with your eyes shall you look, and see the reward of the wicked. Because you have made the LORD, *who* is my refuge, even the Most High, your dwelling place, no evil shall befall you, nor shall any plague come near your dwelling; For He shall give his angels charge over you, to keep you in all your ways. In *their* hands they shall bear you up, lest you dash your foot against a stone. You shall tread upon the lion and the cobra, the young lion and the serpent you shall trample underfoot. "Because he has set his love upon Me, therefore I will deliver him; I will set him on high, because he has known My name. He shall call upon Me, and I will answer him; I *will be* with him in trouble; I will deliver him and honor him. With long life I will satisfy him, and show him my salvation." (Psalm 91)

If you should slip my friend, remember that there is no condemnation for those who are in Christ Jesus. Simply repent. And keep a short account with God. Don't wait to confess your sin to Him. He loves you and is rich in mercy, but don't take Him for granted. Grace is not a licence to sin; it is a gift and the empowering you need to walk out your righteousness. Believe that God has already transformed your identity at its core; you are already the righteousness of Christ. You are already a new creation. Believe it and you will be able to walk it out.

---

[24] From Isaiah11:2 we see 7 facets of the Holy Spirit: the Spirit of the Lord, the Spirit of Wisdom, the Spirit of Understanding, the Spirit of Counsel, the Spirit of Might, the Spirit of Knowledge and the Spirit of the Fear of the Lord. Other examples are the Spirit of Truth, the Spirit of Discernment, the Spirit of Revelation, the Spirit of Repentance, the Spirit of Mercy, the Spirit of Kindness etc.

[25] Proverbs 18:10, Psalms 18:2-3, Psalms 144:2, 2 Samuel 22:2-4, Psalms 32:7

[26] Harlotry is not just exchanging sex for money; it is when we depart from the Lord, commit idolatry and adultery against God as we chase after "lesser lovers." Hosea 1:2 says, "When the LORD began to speak by Hosea, the LORD said to Hosea: "Go, take yourself a wife of harlotry and children of harlotry, for the land has committed great harlotry by departing from the LORD.""

CONCLUSION

Mercy and grace. What a gift! Freedom from torment. Freedom from sin. Freedom to enjoy the Lord's love and peace. It's so precious. Life in this world is far from perfect, but we do not need to suffer through continuous loss, grief, strife, and heartache which is sure to follow us if we don't repent and steward what God has given us. We have His Word which tells us how to be free. We *can* live here and now in the blessing of the Lord and in His strength if we do our part in His salvation plan: submit to God, repent, and resist the devil by renouncing agreement with darkness and commanding the devil and his minions to go.

For so long, many of you have not been filled up with the pure, unadulterated, love of God. You have been trying to survive half empty, trying to get filled up with the wrong things—looking for love in all the wrong places because your heart has been half-dead, numb, and unable to receive. You have relied on sex and physical sensations to feel love. But God has so much more for you now. Now, I see sisters who are running through fields of wildflowers soaking in the rays of the sun like they've never felt them before. I see sisters who are feeling the warmth and tenderness of the love of God for the first time. I see the Lord picking a bouquet of wildflowers for you and placing one in your hair. And God says, "Let me fill your tank. Let me love you like you've never been loved before. Come away with me. Come away into my chambers and let me hold you… let me look into your eyes and behold you. Linger with me. Stay a while. And let me fill your heart. Let me sustain you."

Friends, listen to Song of Songs, parts of chapter one. I did not read this until after I wrote what is above.

> The Woman: Let him kiss me with the kisses of his mouth—for your love is more delightful than wine. Pleasing is the fragrance of your perfumes; your name is like perfume poured out. No wonder the young women love you! Take me away with you—let us hurry! *Let the king bring me into his chambers.* (Song of Songs 1:2-4 NIV)

> When my King-Lover lay down beside me, my fragrance filled the room. His head resting between my breasts—the head of my lover was a sachet of sweet myrrh. *My beloved is a bouquet of wildflowers picked just for me* from the fields of En Gedi. (Song of Songs 1:12-14 MSG, emphasis added)

The love the Lord wants you to receive is an intimate love. It's not physically sexual but it is intimate... personal... close... sweet... delicate... and meant to be private, just between you and Him. He wants you to feel completely known, seen, and accepted just as you are, flaws and all.

I pray that you have found the freedom you need in the arms of Christ.

Let me conclude with 2 Peter 1:2-11 as follows:

> May God give you more and more grace and peace as you grow in your knowledge of God and Jesus our Lord. By his divine power, God has given us everything we need for living a godly life. We have received all of this by coming to know him, the one who called us to himself by means of his marvelous glory and excellence. And because of his glory and excellence, he has given us great and precious promises. These are the promises that enable you

> to share his divine nature and escape the world's corruption caused by human desires. In view of all this, make every effort to respond to God's promises. Supplement your faith with a generous provision of moral excellence, and moral excellence with knowledge, and knowledge with self-control, and self-control with patient endurance, and patient endurance with godliness, and godliness with brotherly affection, and brotherly affection with love for everyone. The more you grow like this, the more productive and useful you will be in your knowledge of our Lord Jesus Christ. But those who fail to develop in this way are shortsighted or blind, forgetting that they have been cleansed from their old sins. So, dear brothers and sisters, work hard to prove that you really are among those God has called and chosen. Do these things, and you will never fall away. Then God will give you a grand entrance into the eternal Kingdom of our Lord and Savior Jesus Christ. (NLT)

May the Lord bless you and keep you. May He cause His face to shine on you and be gracious to you. May He turn His face toward you and give you peace (Numbers 6:24-26).

I declare over you today that because of your obedience and submission to the Lord, He is restoring completely the purity of your marriage bed… that He is sprinkling the blood of His Son over your heart, your eyes, and on your bed to fully redeem what's been lost. He is orchestrating the final touches on His marvelous and glorious plan for your life and intimate relationship with your hubby to bring it back to the original intentions of His heart.

Cry out with me, friends! "Lord, make our hearts soft toward our husbands and make his heart soft toward us. Do what only You can do! Smooth out the rough edges and take the walls down."

Thank you, sister, for the privilege of speaking into your life. It is an honor I do not take lightly.

All God's best be yours, in Jesus' name.

APPENDIX A

ARE YOU TRULY RE-BORN AND SAVED?

Jesus and our relationship with Him are our firm foundation for abundant life. There are three elements that are needed to establish an intimate relationship with Jesus and keep it strong. They are, an *authentic transformation* of the heart resulting in re-birth and salvation, the *empowerment* of the Holy Spirit through *the baptism* of the Holy Spirit (Appendix B) and being able to hear (Appendix C) and follow the voice of the Lord in obedience.

Unfortunately, the church in many main-line denominations have done a dis-service to people by teaching that a simple prayer recited somehow leads to salvation. The traditional *pray after me* scenario has led some people to a moment where they have recited words without having their heart engaged or have given their mental ascent to the gospel but have not given their heart in love to Jesus; they have not had a revelation of Who Jesus is nor of His love for them. This *may* have led some people to think they are saved, when *perhaps* they really aren't.

Jesus is coming back for a *bride*. He is not coming back for *just* friends or *just* servants, nor those that simply believe in Him. He is coming back for a *bride* who is in *love* with Him. So, as a quick evaluation of your own heart, do you *love* Jesus? Are you in love with Him? Jesus said in John 14:21, "Those who accept my commandments and obey them are the ones who love me. And because they love me, my Father will love them. And I will love them and reveal myself to each of them" (NLT).

A true salvation experience begins with a revelation of one's need, a revelation of one's own sin and brokenness. It continues with a revelation from the Holy Spirit of Jesus and His sacrifice for us personally, then a revelation of the goodness and kindness of God which then causes a person to fall in love with Jesus and on their knees in repentance.[27] A true salvation experience is a change of heart *and* mind causing someone to stop and turn around, changing direction. It causes a person who is unknowingly headed for a cliff, to adjust their course so they turn around and head back to the arms of God. And it's this call back to God, back to love, that instigates and perpetuates a change in desires, through the Spirit, which leads to a change in behavior. Holiness is *not* an act of the human will. It is *not* striving and pulling up your bootstraps, *trying* to do better. It is a change of heart and transformation of the soul initiated and perpetuated by the Holy Spirit, *as we yield to Him*.

Let's be real about our walk with God, Christian. Are you *really* a *follower* of Christ? Have you *really surrendered* your life, every bit of it, even your will, to Jesus? A Christian is a *follower* of Christ which means they watch what Jesus does, and by the empowering of the Holy Spirit, they imitate Him. They think how Christ thinks. They say what Christ says. To some degree, they are "little Christs." They may not do it perfectly yet, but their desire is to get there. They are grieved by their sin and how they fall short, and they live a life of repentance when they do. They *love* Jesus with all their heart. They don't just believe in Him (even the devil believes in Him). Born-again believers *love* Him. They sacrifice for Him. They give things up to *do* His Word. They live a life of service, and they are obedient to Christ. They long to be with Him.

Love for, trust in, and surrender to Jesus is a huge part of the foundation that we must have to experience relationship and intimacy with God, and to encounter His presence. Don't settle for less my friend. Seek the Holy Spirit and ask

Him to bring you *all* the way in. *Surrender* your life afresh today. I pray the Holy Spirit captures your heart through these words. It is *not* His desire for you or anyone else to perish[28] nor to live one more day without His *discernable*, *abiding* presence.

---

[27] "… the goodness of God leads you to repentance" (Romans 2:4b NKJV)?

[28] "In the same way, it is not my heavenly Father's will that even one of these little ones should perish" (Matthew 18:14 NLT).

APPENDIX B

BAPTISM IN THE HOLY SPIRIT

After we have authentically surrendered ourselves to the authority of Christ, repented for our sin, and made a decision to turn from it, a second experience as outlined in the New Testament called the baptism of the Holy Spirit[29] is crucial for numerous reasons. Being baptized in the Holy Spirit causes our spiritual senses to awaken, giving us the potential to discern in the Spirit. As we exercise our spiritual senses, they will develop, and we will gain wisdom and understanding from God's perspective being able to "distinguish between what is morally good and what is evil" (Hebrews 5:14b AMP). We will read our Bible and get it. We will grow in our ability to recognize God's voice and discern His presence. And we will be empowered to overcome temptation and any other nonsense the devil throws at us.

As we yield to the Holy Spirit, we will experience a deeper prayer life. We will hear the Holy Spirit direct us on how to pray and what to pray, so we are praying God's heart and not our own soulish desires. As we continue to yield, we can even begin to experience a new prayer language which is private and intimate between us and God. Best of all, we will begin to feel the love of God like never before and we will go from a Christian life that is just theory to a wonderful life of *experiencing* God. God will come alive to us! This is the beauty of being baptized in the Holy Spirit and it pains me to know so many Christians miss out because their church or denomination chooses to ignore it.

What does it mean to be *baptized* in the Holy Spirit? I would suggest to you that it means being fully immersed in, saturated by, inside and out, and completely filled to overflowing with the Holy Spirit and His power. Once we're baptized and filled, it is then our job to yield to Him and give Him control.

This I think is the sticking point for some people. They see giving control over to the Spirit as not having control over themselves. This is a misunderstanding; it's not one or the other. God never overrides our free will. We always have the choice to yield or not to yield in any given moment. God is good. God has our *best* interest at heart. He never forces Himself on us and He never forces us to do anything we don't want to do. He may nudge us out of our comfort zones, and want us to obey, but the final choice is always ours. He knows our heart completely and He is so very patient with us. It really comes down to trust. Do we trust God enough to give His Spirit the reigns of our life?

John the Baptist said in Matthew 3:11, "I indeed baptize you with water unto repentance, but He who is coming after me is mightier than I, whose sandals I am not worthy to carry. He will baptize you with the Holy Spirit and fire" (NKJV). We know from this passage that Jesus is the One to baptize us with the Holy Spirit. It is worthy to note also that the Holy Spirit was imparted to the disciples twice—once with an emphasis on internal awakening and once with the addition of external equipping and empowerment. *Baptism* in the Holy Spirit causes one to not only be filled but to "wear" the Holy Spirit on the outside, equipped with Godly fire, passion, and power. The two instances of the disciples receiving the Holy Spirit are as follows:

1. John 20:19-22. After Jesus' resurrection, Jesus appeared to his disciples showing them his pierced hands and side. He commissioned them and *breathed* on them saying, "Receive the Holy Spirit." Jesus breathed on them with the intent of imparting the Holy Spirit to them. As Jesus

breathed out, they breathed IN what Jesus released—the Holy Spirit. This impartation represents what happens for believers at their re-birth—the Spirit causes their human spirit to come alive spiritually.

2. Acts 1:5. The infilling (complete saturation) of the Holy Spirit happened at Pentecost and represents the *baptism* of the Holy Spirit which includes the enduement of power and the Holy Spirit resting ON them. Jesus gave the apostles instruction to remain in Jerusalem and wait for the "gift" His Father promised: "For John baptized with water, but you will be baptized and empowered and united with the Holy Spirit, not long from now" (Acts 1:5 AMP). The apostles waited in Jerusalem for the Holy Spirit to come, as they were instructed. In due time, the Holy Spirit came spontaneously just as Jesus said He would:

    > Suddenly a sound like the blowing of a violent wind came from heaven and filled the whole house where they were sitting. They saw what seemed to be tongues of fire that separated and came to *rest on* each of them. All of them were filled with the Holy Spirit and began to speak in other tongues as the Spirit enabled them (Acts 2:2-4 NIV, emphasis added).

The baptism in the Holy Spirit can happen spontaneously as you believe, surrender, open your heart to Him, and ask to be filled *and* empowered. It can happen as you read these words right now or as an anointed leader imparts the Spirit to you by the laying on of hands, or as you listen to the Word being preached at church, in your car and even at home. The key is your desire for Him. But it does not necessarily happen for everyone when they believe; it is very often a second experience from salvation, depending on if you seek Him or have someone laying hands on you praying for it on your behalf.

We see Jesus being spontaneously baptized in the Holy Spirit right after His water baptism in Matthew 3:16, "After his baptism, as Jesus came up out of the water, the heavens were opened, and he saw the Spirit of God descending like a dove and settling *on him*" (NLT, emphasis added). We see new believers being baptized in the Holy Spirit spontaneously as they listen to Peter share the Gospel in Acts 10:44 and we see others being baptized in the Holy Spirit with the laying on of hands in Acts 8:17 and Acts 19:6 after their decision to believe and water baptism.

The Holy Spirit is not just for certain denominations. He is for everyone, and we need Him to connect to God. God is Spirit and in order to worship God, we must worship in Spirit.[30] If we want to approach the throne of grace in our time of need, we can only do so in the Spirit.[31] Obviously, the throne of God is not in the natural, it is in the spiritual realm. Partnering with the Holy Spirit is not an option, if we want to function as a Christian who is alive, aware, walking in the things of God, hearing His voice, and receiving healing.

Robert Boyd Munger has written a very well-known devotional booklet called, *My Heart: Christ's Home*. You may have heard of it. This devotional introduces readers to what it means to surrender every aspect of their lives to the control of Christ by comparing our heart to a home. I've actually not read it in its entirety, but I love the idea. Using this comparison, imagine that salvation (repenting, believing, confessing, and surrendering), is like inviting Christ into our home, through the front door.

The front door is the entrance way, and the Lord has come in. He has brought life and light back into our home, but where does He reside? Does He just stay in the foyer or is He welcomed into *every* room? Is He restricted to the formal living room where things are in order or is He free to roam—to open closets and cupboards and look under the bed? Is He treated like a guest or like He belongs there? Is He treated like part of the family or is He treated properly—like He's the head of the house—like He's in charge?

Perhaps Jesus is honored well, given access to every room, and received as the authority figure in the home, but what about the Holy Spirit? The Holy Spirit is not synonymous with Jesus; they are two separate members of the Godhead with different assignments, functions, and roles in our lives. So, do we invite the Holy Spirit in and honor Him the same way we honor Jesus, as we should?

Here's what I fear happens in denominations that don't believe in the *baptism* of the Holy Spirit: they open the door, and the Holy Spirit comes in, but they immediately stuff Him into the front hall closet, not permitting Him to move, fill the house nor do any of what He desires to do—such as heal, comfort, transform and communicate truth.

Unfortunately, some Christians don't trust the supernatural demonstrations of God through the Holy Spirit as it feels strange, out of control, and they can't understand it with their natural minds. It offends their flesh. However, we all must allow our mind and experience to be governed by the Spirit, not the flesh. Romans 8:6-8 says the following:

> The mind governed by the flesh is death, but the mind governed by the Spirit is life and peace. The mind governed by the flesh is hostile to God; it does not submit to God's law, nor can it do so. Those who are in the realm of the flesh cannot please God. (NIV)

Friends, to experience the supernatural love of God, we are going to have to be willing to experience His supernatural Spirit. We should not be afraid to let the Holy Spirit do what He wants to do. He wants to bless us outrageously and heal us on the inside and out.

I have had some of the most profound, amazing healing experiences flat on my back, on the floor, completely overtaken by the power of God, as the Holy Spirit has ministered to me through visions on the screen of my imagination. He has taken me back to some very painful and traumatic experiences and brought me through them again amidst His presence, completely changing my memory of them. The only reason it was possible for God to do this for me was because I was willing to submit to Him. I was willing to give the Holy Spirit control.

If you have been fearful or prideful or not honoring of the Holy Spirit, repent and ask God to forgive you. Then, open your heart to receive and simply ask God for His gift of the Spirit. Do not be shy. Jesus tells us in Luke 11 to ask for the Holy Spirit and to keep on asking.

> And so I tell you, keep on asking, and you will receive what you ask for. Keep on seeking, and you will find. Keep on knocking, and the door will be opened to you. For everyone who asks, receives. Everyone who seeks, finds. And to everyone who knocks, the door will be opened. You fathers—if your children ask for a fish, do you give them a snake instead? Of if they ask for an egg, do you give them a scorpion? Of course not! So if you sinful people know how to give good gifts to your children, how much more will your heavenly Father give the Holy Spirit to those who ask him (Luke 11:9-13 NLT).

We can even ask repeatedly. In fact, I would encourage every believer to continually ask for more of the Holy Spirit. You will find that as you serve the Lord pouring out to others, you will need to be replenished with His power and presence.

---

[29] "I baptize with water those who repent of their sins and turn to God. But someone is coming soon who is greater than I am—so much greater that I'm not worthy even to be his slave and carry his sandals. He will baptize you with the Holy Spirit and with fire" (Matthew 3:11 NLT).

[30] "God is Spirit, so those who worship him must worship in spirit and in truth" (John 4:24 NLT).

[31] "So let us come boldly to the throne of our gracious God. There we will receive his mercy, and we will find grace to help us when we need it most" (Hebrews 4:16 NLT).

APPENDIX C

HEARING GOD'S VOICE

Hearing the voice of God is necessary for a vibrant relationship with Him. How can we have a relationship with anyone without hearing their voice and being able to talk with them? Jesus declares in the parable of the sheep in John 10 that He is the gate, and He is the good Shepherd who sacrifices His life for the sheep. He also says that His sheep know His voice and follow it.

> I tell you the truth, anyone who sneaks over the wall of a sheepfold, rather than going through the gate, must surely be a thief and a robber! But the one who enters through the gate is the shepherd of the sheep. The gatekeeper opens the gate for him, and the sheep recognize his voice and come to him. He calls his own sheep by name and leads them out. After he has gathered his own flock, he walks ahead of them, and they follow him because they know his voice. They won't follow a stranger; they will run from him because they don't know his voice. . . I am the good shepherd; I know my own sheep, and they know me, just as my Father knows me and I know the Father. So I sacrifice my life for the sheep. I have other sheep too, that are not in this sheepfold. I must bring them also. They will listen to my voice, and there will be one flock with one shepherd (John 10:1-5, 14-16 NLT).

We absolutely have the ability, through the Spirit, to recognize the voice of Jesus our Lord and to be directed by Him. We hear His voice in different ways, but *primarily* through reading His Word, the Bible.

Have you ever noticed that as you read the Bible, occasionally a certain passage, verse, phrase, or word will jump out at you or be highlighted—a portion of what you are reading penetrates your heart with power and reverberates in your inner being? This is an indication that God is bringing that portion of His Word to your attention and is speaking it to you in that moment. You may not be able to identify what's happening, but if you pay close attention, you may notice that it feels like a vibration in your spirit. This is because God's voice is adding sound to the written Words you are reading. The written Word becomes the spoken Word. At this moment, His Word comes alive with power, changing and healing as it defies natural laws, exposing what needs to be exposed, cutting, and dividing what is soulish from what is spirit. Hebrews 4 puts it this way:

> For the word of God is alive and powerful. It is sharper than the sharpest two-edged sword, cutting between soul and spirit, between joint and marrow. It exposes our innermost thoughts and desires. Nothing in all creation is hidden from God. Everything is naked and exposed before his eyes, and he is the one to whom we are accountable (Hebrews 4:12-13 NLT).

Of course, the whole of the written Word is God's Word and is alive, but it is the portion that God wants you to hear in the moment that will pierce you when you need it. And you will just know in your spirit, *there's power on that Word FOR ME right now and I need to receive it, BELIEVE IT, and step into it, to experience the benefits flowing from it.*

Did you know that God created the world simply by speaking? He did not need to hire an architect, or contractor to build anything. He did not need any raw materials. He simply spoke, and it was. "And God said, 'Let there be light'; and there was light" (Genesis 1:3 AMP). The sound of His voice creates. The sound of His voice establishes exactly what He says.

It is incredible what I noticed just the other day in Matthew 14:22-32. Let me share it with you. Jesus sent His disciples out in the boat ahead of Him while He dismissed the crowd that had been listening to Him speak. Later, shortly before dawn, Jesus went out to them walking on the water. Initially the disciples were afraid and thought He was a ghost, but Jesus called out to them, calming their fear.

Peter, the zealous bold one, said to Jesus, "Lord, if it's really you, *tell me to come to you*, walking on the water" (Matthew 14:28 NLT, emphasis added). "'Yes, come.' Jesus said. So, Peter went over the side of the boat and walked on the water toward Jesus" (Matthew 14:29 NLT). I never thought of this too much before, but *Peter asked Jesus to command him to come out on the water* BEFORE he attempted it. He waited for the Word from Jesus. Why? Why not just get out of the boat and go? Well, Peter understood that he needed the Word of the Lord before he could experience supernatural things that defy earthly laws. Peter does not take anything for granted nor does he presume anything. And neither should we. Jesus is the One Who has authority over the natural realm, not us. The natural laws submit to Jesus and His Word. If we need something in the natural realm to shift, we need the Word from Jesus to do it.

The Word of the Lord creates, empowers, releases, and overcomes every earthly limitation. Therefore, we need to read healing scriptures over ourselves. Something we read is going to catch the breath of God, cut through our issue and bring healing. Having said that, I believe also, that just as

Peter asked the Lord to command him to come out on the water, we are invited to ask Jesus to command our healing.

Seeking the Lord in the secret place is vital to hearing Him speak a Word of healing. When I say, "secret place," I mean in a private place and way, so you and the Lord can be together intimately to share your hearts together. Don't just make time to pray quickly in the morning as you dress or drive the car or perhaps when you're doing chores. Seek the Lord INTENTIONALLY, behind closed doors, with NO DISTRACTIONS, and give Him your time. Prioritize a time when you can be set apart to hear Him. Only one Word from Him can create your miracle healing.

In summary, READ the Word and HEAR the Word. When a portion of scripture resonates in your heart, read it over repeatedly and read it aloud. Sit with it. Chew on it. Receive it. Believe it. If there is something you need to do to activate it, do it!

Another common way God speaks to us is through prayer. Did you know that prayer is supposed to be a two-way conversation? Prayer was never meant to be a monologue but a dialogue. I've always loved King David's prayer in Psalm 139:23, "Search me, O God, and know my heart; test me and know my anxious thoughts. Point out anything in me that offends you and lead me along the path of everlasting life" (NLT).

God speaks. He's alive and He has a voice. He is speaking to us ALL the time. Sometimes He speaks through the pages of the Bible and in prayer. Other times He speaks through different things like dreams, books, and songs. Even other times He speaks through people—particularly when you're listening to a sermon online or when someone anointed prays for you or gives you a prophetic word. In addition, you may find God speaks to you through social media or even a billboard!

You may be asking, "How do I know if God is speaking to me when I read a billboard?" That's a good question. It's a little out of the box, isn't it? You will know it's God when it grabs your attention, convicts you, won't leave you alone, and perhaps confirms something you've already been thinking or praying about. Over time, you will begin to recognize His voice, how it makes you feel, and other signs that come with it.

I'll never forget the first time I heard the voice of God in my spirit as I prayed. The Lord answered a question I had asked Him directly, responding with a clear Word of direction. It just about blew my mind.

I was standing at the sink washing dishes and I had just had a healing experience in the car on the way home from Toronto (the same one I shared with you back on page 64-65). After the car ride as I stood at the sink, I had a new sense of peace. The anxiety, hate and emotional pain I had felt previously was gone and I was so thankful. I asked the Lord directly, "What do you want me to do with this now?" and *immediately* I heard God say in my thoughts, "Join the youth group." I was stunned. Becoming an adult sponsor for high schoolers was not even on my radar. It wasn't something I had thought about before. However, I did what God told me to do and I loved it. I became an adult sponsor for the youth group at our church, and it stretched me, caused me to grow and use my spiritual gifts to bless others. It was exactly where God wanted me to be at that time in my life.

One final way I will mention that God speaks is through dreams. This is a whole teaching by itself, but I will say this:

- Everyone has dreams whether we remember them or not.
- Not every dream is from God.
- Dreams from God are vivid and seem very real.
- God speaks in dreams through symbols and what they mean biblically and/or to you.
- Keep a journal by your bedside to journal your dream as soon as you wake up before you forget.
- God dreams can be extremely helpful to you in life as they can contain direct messages from God.
- The Holy Spirit will give you the interpretation of the dream if you ask Him.
- Talking your dream out sometimes gives you clues as to what it means.
- It is biblical (See Job 33:14-15). Daniel and Joseph both interpreted God's messages in dreams.

Several years ago, my daughter was at college and at the end of the school year, as she was getting off the campus bus, she slipped and hit the back of her head on the step. We thought she was fine until she went back to school a few months later and began having severe headaches and difficulty with her memory. She finished the semester, took a break from college, and came home to rest and heal.

Shortly after she returned home, as I sought the Lord on her behalf, I had a dream:

> I was at a college campus in the campus bookstore, and I was in line, waiting to buy a scarf. The scarf was white and on the scarf were two handprints with the words, "They will lift you up." When I reached the cashier, the cashier didn't know how to cash out that particular item, so I helped her out by cashing myself out on the bookstore's register.

I knew the Lord was speaking to me. I was at a college campus, so it was obviously referring to my daughter. She was the only one in the family at college. I was purchasing a scarf that was white which speaks of covering and purity. MY purchasing the scarf was confirmation that I had successfully partnered with God to activate His covering over me and my children. As Jessica's mother, the one in authority over her, my covering translated to her covering. Most powerfully though, the inscription on the scarf pointed me to the Word, Psalm 91:11-12:

> For he will command his angels concerning you to guard you in all your ways; *they will lift you up in their hands*, so that you will not strike your foot against a stone (or your head against a step). (NIV, brackets and emphasis mine)

The next morning as I contemplated the dream and read the scripture, I realized by the Spirit in that moment, that God was actually changing history. As I caught revelation of His breath and voice on that Word from Psalm 91, I saw in my mind's eye, angels slipping their hands underneath my daughter's head as it hit the step, protecting her from the impact. From that moment on, she no longer had severe headaches due to a concussion or problems with her memory. (For more information about how God speaks in dreams, look for resources by Barbie Breathitt or James Goll.)

These are the foundations of connecting with God: an authentic salvation experience of heart transformation, baptism in the Holy Spirit, and hearing His voice followed by obedient action. All three set you up to begin and grow a vibrant, intimate relationship with God, through the Holy Spirit. If you are convicted that you don't have all three of these elements, simply follow the Spirit and re-dedicate your life to Jesus as He leads you. This may look like:

- Surrendering to Jesus afresh and accepting Him again (or for the first time) as your Savior AND Lord.
- Asking God to fill you with the Holy Spirit and new life.
- Asking Jesus to baptize you IN the Holy Spirit to clothe you in His power so you can live for Him, be a witness wherever you go and serve Him well.
- Getting to know God and His heart by reading His Word.
- Memorizing verses that are special to you.
- Praying and expecting to hear God's voice and asking the Lord to help you.
- Giving the Holy Spirit an opportunity to speak to you by asking Him direct questions. Start simple.
- Spending time with God and attuning your ear to the sound of His voice through reading His Word, especially the Gospels where Jesus speaks directly (Matthew, Mark, Luke, and John).
- Allowing the Holy Spirit to pray through you however that looks and sounds.
- Being open to praying in tongues—a heavenly language between you and God. Learn more from a book by John Bevere called, "The Holy Spirit: An introduction."
- Praying in tongues often.
- Joining a church fellowship that teaches biblical principles and a FULL gospel including the Holy Spirit and the activation of all His gifts from 1 Corinthians 12:7-11 in our lives.

ABOUT THE AUTHOR

Barbara Jane grew up in a family of five attending a Christian Science church in London, Ontario until the age of twenty-two when the Lord, Jesus, called her into His fold. She has now never been so grateful for the transformation the Lord began in her life in that moment of revelation and salvation. It was a moment when everything clicked into place and everything she knew about God became crystal clear and made sense; the revelation of Jesus Christ was the missing piece. The years that followed would prove to be life altering and internally transforming in many ways.

Through her thirty-six years of faith in Christ thus far, she has had to face and renounce many things that tainted her family line like the antichrist spirit, the spirit of error and deception, lies, abuse in many forms, deep anger, hate, unforgiveness, bitter judgements, vows to self, disappointment, rejection, self-loathing, and despair. As she has walked out of agreement with darkness, breakthrough has been had in different areas of life including her ability to conceive and bear natural children. Because of the goodness and healing of the Lord, Barbara Jane had four amazing children—one beautiful girl and three handsome boys, who are now all thriving adults. In addition, she and her husband now have a wonderful daughter-in-law who makes a lovely addition to their original four.

It is with great honor that Barbara Jane pours out to her readers the knowledge, wisdom, and understanding that the Lord has poured into her. And it is her prayer that the time, love, and effort she has put into her books brings about great blessing and transformation in the lives of others. There is nothing more gratifying to Barbara than being used of the Lord to assist the Bride of Christ in getting ready for her big day of finally becoming perfectly united with her bridegroom, Jesus Christ.

Barbara has had the privilege of sitting under Apostle Barbara Yoder's teaching for a time and is connected to Patricia King's Women in Ministry Network. Barbara is also part of a local Pentecostal Assemblies of Canada church.

Barbara has written the following books available on Amazon:

Barren No More: Prayer Strategy for Every Believer Experiencing Fertility Challenges

Key to Fertility: Rewriting Your Stories for Success in Conceiving and Birthing Babies

Sweet Sorrow: Surviving the Emotional Waves of Releasing Your Son to His Bride

Position Yourself for Healing: Finding the Sweet Spot Where Healing Becomes Reality (Third Edition now available)

Spiritual Protection and Deliverance for our Children

Loved and Fully Surrendered

Walking in the Spirit: 12 Days Hearing God Through Psalm 139

Running in the Spirit: 12 Days Hearing God Through Psalm 139 for Men

www.ingramcontent.com/pod-product-compliance
Lightning Source LLC
LaVergne TN
LVHW010719061126
851857LV00014B/1253
* 9 7 8 1 7 3 8 3 8 4 0 9 9 *